CHOP
SUEY
NATION

ANN HUI

CHOP SUEY NATION

THE LEGION CAFE AND OTHER STORIES
FROM CANADA'S CHINESE RESTAURANTS

Douglas & McIntyre

Douglas and McIntyre (2013) Ltd.
P.O. Box 219, Madeira Park, BC, V0N 2H0
www.douglas-mcintyre.com

All photos courtesy of Ann Hui/*The Globe and Mail* except where otherwise noted.

Edited by Nicola Goshulak
Cover and text design by Diane Robertson
Printed and bound in Canada
Printed on paper made from 100% post-consumer waste

Douglas and McIntyre (2013) Ltd. acknowledges the support of the Canada Council for the Arts, which last year invested $153 million to bring the arts to Canadians throughout the country.

Nous remercions le Conseil des arts du Canada de son soutien. L'an dernier, le Conseil a investi 153 millions de dollars pour mettre de l'art dans la vie des Canadiennes et des Canadiens de tout le pays.

We also gratefully acknowledge financial support from the Government of Canada and from the Province of British Columbia through the BC Arts Council and the Book Publishing Tax Credit.

Canada

Canada Council   Conseil des Arts
for the Arts   du Canada

BRITISH COLUMBIA
ARTS COUNCIL
An agency of the Province of British Columbia

LIBRARY AND ARCHIVES CANADA CATALOGUING IN PUBLICATION

Hui, Ann, 1983-, author

   Chop suey nation : the Legion Cafe and other stories from Canada's Chinese restaurants / Ann Hui.

Includes bibliographical references.
Issued in print and electronic formats.

ISBN 978-1-77162-222-6 (softcover).--ISBN 978-1-77162-223-3 (HTML)

   1. Chinese restaurants--Canada. 2. Cooking, Chinese. 3. Cooking, Canadian. 4. Food habits--Canada. I. Title.

TX945.4.H85 2019   647.9571   C2018-906139-1
                                        C2018-906140-5

for Dad

Table of Contents

Author's Note

THIS BOOK IS based on interviews and many of the events described have been reconstructed from memories of what took place decades ago. I have attempted to be as accurate as possible in compiling these memories. But as with all family histories, this one is messy, and it is possible that some of the details may have been misremembered. Also, for the sake of consistency, for people living in Canada, I have followed Canadian usage in writing their given name preceding their surname.

Introduction

UNTIL THE YEAR I turned nine, my family lived in the house across the street from our school. On one side of Franklin Street was the beige building where we attended classes. And on the other side was the white stucco house where we grew up.

When the bell rang at noon each day, while everyone else ran off to the cafeteria or playground, my sisters and I went home for lunch. The three of us would walk across the street to find Mom cooking, usually fried noodles or fried rice. We'd walk in to see her cracking eggs and mixing them up with a pair of chopsticks for the fried rice. Into the wok she'd drop cold rice from the night before. Then she'd cut up some green onions and throw those in too. I hated green onions.

I was jealous of my friends who got to stay at school for lunch. I was jealous of their brightly coloured lunch boxes covered with cartoons and Disney princesses, and the fact that they got to eat lunch together. If they ate quickly, they could call dibs on the best swings and slides and have plenty of time on the playground. At home, Mom kept a stern eye on us as we ate. No one was allowed out the door and back to the playground until she could see the bottom of our bowls.

I was jealous of what was inside my friends' lunch boxes too. They ate the same things as the characters in our favourite TV shows: neatly wrapped bologna and cheese sandwiches. Tupperware containers filled with SpaghettiOs or tomato soup. Little plastic packets filled with Fruit Roll-Ups or Minigo. It was the food they sold at Safeway and advertised in cartoon commercials. *Normal* food.

The food we ate at home was something different. It was the same kind of different I felt when the white girls in class had sleepover parties, and I'd lie and say my family and I were out of town. Chinese families didn't do sleepovers.

It was the same kind of different I felt when friends would talk about Saturday morning cartoons. I'd nod along knowingly as if I knew my *Darkwing Duck* from my *DuckTales*. In reality, I was at Chinese school every Saturday morning, practising dictation and learning classical Chinese poetry.

One day in third grade, a girl in my class, Cherie, turned to me on the playground after I came back from lunch. "What'd you eat?" she asked. Cherie was my friend but I was intimidated by her. She was Chinese too. But I'd never seen her at Chinese school. I'd never seen her eating slimy noodles with pickled vegetables, or the soy-marinated duck wings I loved even though some of the hairs were often still poking out. Cherie ate sandwiches and wore sweatshirts with the real, licenced Care Bears and Fido Dido images on them. She didn't wear the knock-off stuff that relatives brought back to Vancouver in suitcases from Hong Kong, the way we did. I imagined her parents spoke perfect, fluent English.

I froze, feeling like I'd been caught. Like most days, we'd had fried rice with leftovers.

"Sandwiches," I lied. My face felt hot as I turned away, hoping she wouldn't ask anything more.

Making matters worse, our lunches weren't very good. Mom wasn't a good cook. She thought nothing of mixing together leftovers that had no business being mixed together. She would throw together whatever was in the refrigerator: preserved salted vegetables—pickled and salty and straight from the can—with black-bean and garlic spareribs from the night before. Or add cold cuts Dad brought home from work into fried rice with dried oysters.

She just didn't care very much. Between working nights at the post office and taking care of the three of us—shuttling us around to our piano lessons, swimming classes and kung fu competitions—putting meals on the table was just another thing to check off the list. Food, to her, was simply a necessity. Flavour and pleasure were luxuries she didn't have time for.

Pansy and Amber, my older sisters, were less picky. Most days, they would gobble up their lunches and run out the door before I was even halfway through. (Other times, Amber, who is two years older and more shrewd, would stuff little grains of rice wherever she could think to, most often the porous edge of the table. Every so often, Mom would watch, bewildered, as the dried grains fell from the table's edge, hitting the floor like raindrops.)

That would leave me by myself, drawing shapes and circles on the bottom of my bowl with the tips of my chopsticks. I'd gaze longingly toward the school playground, watching my sisters and my friends running around.

Whining never helped. I knew from experience what would happen if I complained, the look Mom would give me, the flash of anger in her eyes and the words that would soon follow: "*Lup lup gay sun foo.*"

Each and every single grain, from hardship comes.

· · · · · · ·

Still, there was one day of the year when we were allowed to stay at school for lunch: Chinese New Year. Our school cafeteria didn't have a daily meal program, but once a month students could order a special item that was delivered straight to the cafeteria. There was Pizza Day, Hamburger Day and Taco Day. And every year, sometime in January or February, there was Chinese Day, to celebrate Chinese New Year. On that day and only that day, Mom made an exception and allowed us to stay at school. "The school is honouring our culture," she said. "It's a chance to celebrate our heritage."

The first Chinese lunch I can remember, I was about six. I had looked forward to this day for weeks. Finally, I could stay at school like everyone else. I could eat in the cafeteria like everyone else. And my food would be the same as everyone else's.

That afternoon, when the bell rang for lunch, I rushed to the cafeteria, my heart beating with anticipation. For once, *my* food was the kind kids were getting excited about. For that one day at least, *my* lunch would be normal. As I stood in line at the cafeteria, I imagined the meal they'd have waiting for us. There would be fish, surely—every Chinese New Year meal had fish. I could explain to my friends what Mom had told us, how the word for "fish" in Cantonese was a homophone for "excess" or "wealth." It was lucky.

There would be chicken too, probably with the head still on. A whole chicken for Chinese New Year represented wholeness—a good beginning and end for the entire year. And dense, waxy *leen goh,* New Year's cake made of glutinous rice flour and brown sugar. Once cooked, it was wobbly and stuck to our teeth, nothing like the cake we ate at birthdays. This one might scare my friends. But it was one of my favourites, oily from the egg batter Dad fried it in and sweet. Once my friends tried it, I knew they would like it.

The line trudged on until finally it was my turn. The cafeteria worker passed me my plate and I looked down. There was no fish or chicken or *leen goh*—none of the Chinese New Year dishes I knew.

I barely recognized anything on the plate. There were noodles stained dark with soy sauce, limp-looking and glistening with oil. There was nothing mixed in with them except a few pallid bean sprouts. Next to the noodles was some kind of meat, deep-fried with a crunchy exterior and slicked in a fire truck–red sauce. I dipped my finger into the sauce and licked it. It tasted like the red Sugus candies Po Po, my grandmother, kept in a tin above the refrigerator.

None of these foods looked like anything we ate at home. As my friends buzzed around, laughing and shrieking, I could only sit there, baffled. The banner in the cafeteria called this "Chinese" lunch. The school had called it "Chinese" too. So why had I never seen it before? Whose "Chinese" food was this?

Those first few bites, I realized much later, were my introduction to Chinese-Canadian, or "chop suey," cuisine. For years after, I would hear relatives, including Mom and Dad, belittle this as "fake" Chinese. They would tell me that I should only want the *authentic* stuff. I would hear that this was food invented to "trick" Westerners. That it was cheap, or poor quality. That the flavours were garish and lacking in refinement. Other times, relatives would say that chop suey was the only kind of Chinese that non-Chinese people would eat because the *real* stuff would scare them. Those relatives would tell me that our food was too slimy or gristly or strange for others to bear.

Either way, I would hear over and over that this chop suey cuisine had little to do with Chineseness—and certainly nothing to do with us.

What I didn't realize at the time was that this food would eventually grow into a lifelong obsession. And what I *really* didn't realize was that this foreign food had more to do with me than I could ever imagine.

Staring down at my plate that day—the cherry-coloured pork and deep-fried spring rolls—I never could have imagined that these peculiar dishes might one day help me uncover my own story.

Victoria, BC.

Spring 2016

O N A GREY Monday in March, I stepped out of the Victoria International Airport wearing my winter jacket and carrying a suitcase. Hours earlier, my husband Anthony and I had boarded a six a.m. flight from our home in Toronto to Vancouver. From there, we had transferred onto a smaller jet that took us to Victoria.

Our plan was to drive across Canada in eighteen days.

Planning for the trip had begun many months earlier. During a story meeting with my editors at *The Globe and Mail*, I mentioned my interest in Chinese restaurants. I was especially interested, I said, in the "chop suey" style restaurants I saw all over the country.

"There's tons of great, authentic Chinese food all over the country," I said. "And yet this 'chop suey' stuff—this *not*-Chinese Chinese is still everywhere. Why?"

One of the editors, Denise Balkissoon, was immediately intrigued. She encouraged me to develop the idea and so over the course of the next few weeks, we brainstormed questions that the story might answer.

I wanted to understand how so many of these "chop suey" restaurants were so astonishingly similar. At the chop suey restaurants I'd visited in BC's interior, in southwestern Ontario and rural Quebec, "Chinese" somehow looked and felt exactly the same. Somehow, the restaurants all seemed to have the same red vinyl chairs, the same red-tasselled hanging lanterns, the same paper menus, often printed on placemats, always printed in the same font.

I also wanted to know how these chop suey restaurants were doing amid the massive influx of Chinese immigrants to cities like Toronto and Vancouver and their suburbs. The past few decades had introduced Canada to so many different kinds of Chinese—new waves of immigration from all over China, bringing with them very good, very *authentic* regional Chinese food. No longer was it just Cantonese, but also Sichuan or Fujian or Hakka—so many varieties that it no longer made sense to talk about "eating Chinese." Instead, it was Malaysian-Chinese, or Shanghainese, or Hong-Kong-cafe Chinese, or congee-and-noodle Chinese, or Chinatown-small-plate-Edison-bulb Chinese.

I was curious what all these different types of Chinese food meant for the chop suey stuff. I wanted to know: with so much *real* Chinese food available, were people still eating the *fake* stuff?

I also wanted to know what life was like for those running these restaurants. There was one restaurant that captured my imagination, right from the start. I'd stumbled across it on the

Internet, in a blog post titled "I can't believe there's a Chinese restaurant in Fogo." The post was about Fogo Island, the tiny island off the northeastern tip of Newfoundland. The post described a woman living alone, running a Chinese restaurant in the middle of nowhere. For miles around, she was the only Chinese person in sight. Her life seemed about as isolated as I could possibly imagine. I wanted to understand what would compel someone to live a life like hers.

The question I was looking to answer was simple. It was a question I would repeat over and over as I made my way from coast to coast, visiting the many restaurants and explaining the purpose of my visit.

The question was this: How did you wind up here? What brought you here?

· · · · · · ·

I forget when, exactly, but at some point my editors and I decided the trip would have to be a cross-country one. After all, as far as we could tell, every small town across the country seemed to have one of these restaurants.

And so I began planning.

I ruled out flying right away. Flying wouldn't get me to where I needed to go. I was interested in small towns, not cities with giant airports in them. I liked the idea of a train. After all, the railway was what brought many of the Chinese to this country to begin with. But travel by train would be slow. Plus, it would mean I'd be bound by schedules.

So driving seemed like the best option. There was one

problem: I hate driving. But Anthony surprised me by volunteering to come along. By happenstance, he had stumbled upon some free time and was keen to join me on what was shaping up to be a trip of a lifetime. Here was a chance for us to explore together all the nooks and crannies of this country, all the places we might never otherwise think to go see.

He would do the driving, of course. Anthony loves to drive. When we'd first met almost eight years earlier, one of the first things he bragged about wasn't his job, or his car, or any of the usual stuff. It was about his driving ability. And he'd been right to. I'm stressed and anxious behind the wheel, but he's calm and collected. His driving is smooth, effortless. Once, when I was working in Victoria for the summer, he drove from Toronto to Victoria and back again. Together, we'd driven through most of the northeastern US, all the way up and down the Pacific coast and across parts of Europe. No matter where we've been, he's always known how to get where we needed to be.

So it was settled. We would do the trip together. And he would do most (or all) of the driving.

We would drive from coast to coast, we decided. I wanted to go north too, but that would have made the trip longer and even more expensive. With my fixation on Fogo Island, it made sense to save that stop for last. So it seemed logical to begin the trip on the opposite coast, in British Columbia. After all, BC was where the first major wave of Chinese men arrived in Canada in search of gold. When the men disembarked from their long boat journeys back in 1858, Victoria would have been their very first glimpse of this new world.

BC was also where I'd grown up—where my own story began. It would be nice to start the trip somewhere familiar.

• • • • • • •

Outside the airport, Anthony and I waited for the shuttle bus to take us to the car rental office. Even though it was technically already spring, it was cloudy and cool, and I was grateful I'd decided at the last moment to bring my wool coat.

Growing up, I'd visited Victoria from time to time. On school trips, I'd gone on tours of the provincial legislature or to the Royal BC Museum. Later, in my twenties, I spent a summer working as an intern at a local Victoria paper. By day, I'd write news stories about the weather and the local ferry service (the paper loved stories about the local ferry service). And at night I'd hole up in my apartment, sulking about being away from my friends in Toronto. My landlord at the time was an artist whose occasional pot smoke would waft into my apartment through the cracks under the doors, filling the room with the woody, skunky smell.

I'd been struck at the time by how isolated Victoria felt from the rest of the country. I had criss-crossed much of the country by then, visiting all of its major cities in a previous summer job as a flight attendant. But Victoria felt completely removed from what I thought of as the rest of Canada—impossibly far from its centres of power such as Parliament Hill or Bay Street. It felt like a completely different country.

After the shuttle bus dropped us off at the rental car office, we watched as one of the teenaged attendants pulled up in front of us with our car. Instead of the Nissan Versa I had been expecting (the model listed in my reservation), he drove up with a tiny, two-door white Fiat 500.

Anthony and I turned to each other, eyebrows raised.

"I thought I reserved a Nissan Versa?" I said to the woman inside. She glanced at her screen and clicked a few buttons.

"The Fiat is all we have available," she said. "Anything bigger will cost extra."

We went back outside to look again at the car. Anthony is six feet tall. Even with the seats moved all the way back, I wondered where he was supposed to put his legs. The trunk, too, looked impossibly tiny. Although each of us had just the one small carry-on suitcase, I doubted we'd fit them both in there.

Anthony walked up to the car and began testing out the configurations. He pulled the driver and passenger seats all the way back and tested the pedals. He put one of our suitcases in the back seat. Finally, he turned to me and gave me one of his characteristic *it'll-be-fine* shrugs. "We'll make it work."

Inside, the young woman finished her paperwork, punching buttons on her keyboard and preparing the invoice.

"Right now you're paying—" Her voice trailed off, her eyes widening at the total. She scanned the screen again. "No, that can't be right."

I looked at her and sighed. "Yeah, it's right." Instead of the hundreds it would normally cost to rent the car for the eighteen days, the rental company was instead charging us thousands. For the service of picking the car up in BC and dropping it off elsewhere—all the way across the country in Newfoundland—the cost was exponentially higher.

"It's one-way," I told her. "We're driving across the country and dropping the car off in St. John's."

She looked stunned. "You're driving all the way to—" She stopped, the wheels in her head turning. "*Nova Scotia?*"

I didn't bother to correct her. I was too preoccupied with the astonishment on her face.

Her expression said it all: We were about to drive across the entire country—from one ocean to the next, climbing up mountain ranges and navigating rocky terrain—in this tiny toy car?

• • • • • • •

The airport is about thirty minutes north of Victoria. We drove south down Highway 17, making a beeline for Chinatown. The forecast called for rain that afternoon and I wanted to have a chance to walk around before it began to pour.

We drove south along Government Street, rounding the corner at a familiar sight, the red-and-gold archway, the Gate of Harmonious Interest. This was where Chinese immigration first began in Canada.

Before continuing on to the Fraser Valley, gold-seekers had to stop in Victoria for a mining licence. Locals weren't interested in having these men around, so the Chinese set up their own shantytown—crude huts and temporary shacks, sometimes one built on top of another—to stay in until they were ready to continue with their journeys. Over time, some stayed behind to build the area into a neighbourhood of sorts, with services and businesses for these new arrivals: laundries, supply shops and cafes. Chinatown was born.

Decades later, the promise of work on the Canadian Pacific Railway would lure another wave of thousands of Chinese men to Victoria's port, a new boom of Chinese to the country. The Chinese were paid $1 for every $1.50 to $2.50 the white men were paid, and given the most dangerous tasks, such as using explosives to blast through tunnels. And unlike the white men, the Chinese weren't given food or equipment. Many died in accidents, but many more simply died from the cold or malnutrition.

Those who stayed behind in Chinatown didn't have it easy either. Locals saw the cheap labour they provided as a threat. Others blamed the Chinese for what they claimed was an increase in crime and disease. Whether it was out of concern for safety, or for camaraderie and convenience, many of the Chinese men chose to stick together in close geographic quarters as they spread across the country—areas that came to be known as Chinatowns.

In 1887, hundreds of white people led a march through Vancouver's Chinatown, carrying signs reading "Keep Canada White" and "Stop Yellow Peril," and rioting and destroying thousands of dollars' worth of property. In 1907 there was another Vancouver riot, this time with thousands of white men smashing Chinatown windows and again sending residents fleeing.

Responding to these protester's fears, governments across the country put in place laws to restrict the Chinese. Several provinces outlawed Chinese businesses from hiring white women, claiming it would put these women at risk. Many parks and swimming pools banned the Chinese from entering. And in many parts of the country, Chinese were barred from entering most professional occupations, including medicine, law and engineering. So only a few options remained: convenience stores, laundries or restaurants—what was considered "women's work."

We parked and walked over to Fan Tan Alley. Wedged between two brick buildings built just a few feet apart, the narrow passageway led us toward the "hidden" shops and businesses in between. As we wound our way through the alley, a group of tourists posed for photos near the entrance.

During my last summer in Victoria, I had gone on a walking tour of Chinatown with a group of Australian and British tourists. The guide had spent the bulk of the tour here in Fan Tan Alley, conjuring up images of a dark and mysterious society. He'd pointed out the secret passageways, describing how they'd once led to gambling and opium dens—brothels even. "There," he had said, pointing upward at the second-floor balconies, "is where the Chinese men stood on guard on the lookout for police."

His description was partly fair. There *were* brothels and gambling dens in Chinatown—along with all kinds of other businesses.

But what he didn't fully explain was why. He didn't explain how the wages the Chinese men earned working on the railway or at Chinatown businesses were barely enough to support themselves and send money home to their families, let alone enough to bring a wife or a family to Canada. So the Chinatowns became bachelor societies, with gambling and opium emerging as some of the main social activities. (The gambling and opium, in turn, made it even more difficult for some of the men to be able to send money home, creating a vicious cycle.)

The few Chinese women who did live in Canada were either the wives of relatively wealthy merchants, or else women who had been sold into servitude, either as domestic servants or prostitutes.

The Head Tax further cemented this gender imbalance. In 1885 the federal government implemented a fifty-dollar tax on every Chinese person who wanted to enter the country. The tax only applied to the Chinese. And in the following twenty years, the tax would only be increased further and further, peaking at five hundred dollars in 1903. The tax sent a very clear message: that Chinese immigrants were not welcome.

Later, in 1923, the Canadian government took the unprecedented step of banning immigration from China altogether. Canada's Chinese Exclusion Act mimicked a similar policy south of the border. In the US, there was no Head Tax. The US instead implemented a ban on Chinese immigration in 1882 (and eventually repealed that ban in 1943). But Canada took four years longer to repeal its policy—until 1947—and it wouldn't be until the 1960s that Canada began accepting significant numbers of Chinese immigrants.

We continued east along Fisgard, past painted murals of Chinatown's history. In one, a family posed stiffly for a portrait. The man in the centre, Lee Mong Kow, was wearing a blue silk robe and black, Qing-era round court hat. He rose to the position of chief interpreter for Canada's Department of Customs, the plaque read. He was one of the elite few Chinese to have a family in Canada with him. His children, dressed in silk garb, posed in front of him. The boys wore their long hair tied back neatly. I couldn't imagine what the white locals made of these families, with their brightly coloured robes and pigtails. Or what the Chinese thought of the locals.

Just a stone's throw away, a stately brick building stood out, with red lanterns hanging off the pagoda roof in neat rows. I squinted to read the sign: "Chinese Public School." After white locals complained about "unclean" Chinese children attending the same schools as their own, residents of Chinatown set up this school, and it was Lee himself who would serve as its first principal.

The last time I'd visited this Chinatown, I had winced at the carved dragon archways, the little pagodas topping the phone booths and cheap *qipao* for sale everywhere. I was struck by the shops and businesses that seemed to offer only souvenirs for tourists. It had felt like a museum, rather than a working Chinatown. They were selling the *idea* of Chinatown, I complained. I pointed at the coloured paper parasols, Hello Kitty knick-knacks and Japanese kimonos. It was all *fake* Chinese. Even the street signs were printed in that "wonton" font meant to evoke Asia. Meanwhile, the Chinese characters, printed on the street signs on every sidewalk corner, were nonsensical phonetic approximations of the English ones. They looked and sounded Chinese, but didn't actually mean anything. They seemed like the perfect metaphor for this place.

But this time around, I had mellowed. I understood now the fate of other Chinatowns across North America—how many, including Vancouver's, had been left struggling in the wake of Chinese immigration moving instead to the suburbs. In the case of Victoria, many of the city's Chinese left altogether, departing for larger cities such as Vancouver or Toronto. Since the mid-twentieth century, Victoria's Chinese population had been gradually dwindling. So locals banded together, restoring historical buildings in the area and rebranding the area as a tourist destination.

Now, I could see that the Victoria business owners were just being pragmatic and selling what they could to stay afloat.

As we made our way back toward the western edge of Chinatown, we saw how some of the businesses gave up on the "Chineseness" entirely. We walked past old buildings and storefronts that have been converted into hipster coffee shops and offices for tech start-ups.

On the western end of Fisgard was the restaurant I'd been looking for. Both sides of Fisgard were littered with restaurants and shops, but one had always stood out from the rest, with its retro neon signs and flashy decor. We stopped in front of it, taking in the details. The white sign was designed to look like a paper lantern, with the name "Don Mee" etched in a thick black wonton font. Underneath, in red neon lettering: "Seafood," "Szechuan," "Hot Iron Plate." I'd always been curious about the place.

I left Anthony on the sidewalk and hiked up the flight of stairs to the restaurant. The dining room was sprawling, with dozens of tables covered with white tablecloths. The napkins were flame-folded and stuffed into water glasses. Waistcoated servers wandered around the room. It was late afternoon, after the lunch rush, but there were still a few tables with customers in the large dining room. Some were obviously tourists—white couples with guidebooks lying on the table next to them. But there were a few Chinese families there too, having late afternoon dim sum, huddled over cups of tea.

I picked up a menu lying on the counter by the entrance. The restaurant had all the classics of chop suey cuisine: the crispy spring rolls, kung pao chicken and wonton soup. But they also had all the dishes my parents might order. They sold the shredded jellyfish appetizer I loved—cold, springy strands of jellyfish bathed in sesame oil, chili and vinegar. They also had the fish maw soup my sisters and I hated growing up, not because it was made of fish bladders, which we didn't even realize, but because the spongy, chewy texture reminded us of dish towels. It was a *delicacy*, Mom and Dad claimed.

In my mind, a Chinese restaurant had always been one or the other—*authentic* or not. But Don Mee seemed to be both. The restaurant had weathered over eighty years in Victoria. It had seen many generations of Chinese immigration and many versions of Chinatown. And whether by design or out of self-preservation, the restaurant had reinvented itself over and over again.

The middle-aged woman standing behind the counter eyed me up and down, glancing between my business card and my airplane-rumpled appearance. I spoke to her in English first, then switched to Cantonese when I saw her confused expression. I told her the reason I was there and my plans to cross the rest of the country to visit Chinese restaurants just like this one. She wrinkled her brow, staring at me skeptically.

At last, she spoke. "Everybody here is busy and working," she said in Cantonese. "Someone will call you."

The look she gave me reminded me of the young woman at the rental car desk, that mixture of amusement and skepticism. It was clear that nobody was going to call.

As I walked out of the restaurant, I wondered how many other restaurant owners would wind up responding to me in the same way

As a reporter, it was a doubt I was already well acquainted with. It was a question I thought about often—each time I approached a new community and asked to speak with its leaders. A question I thought about each time I asked to speak with someone who had nothing to gain by speaking with me.

And it was a question I knew I would carry with me into every one of these restaurants. When the restaurant owners first set eyes on me, they would see in me someone who looked a little bit like them. But from the moment I introduced myself, they might also see the opportunities I'd been given that they hadn't. I was born in Canada. I grew up speaking English. I got to go to university, then graduate school. In most cases, we were only a single generation apart. But I had been given so much. And now I was walking into their lives and asking for more.

Who was I to walk in and demand to know people's stories?

Burnaby, BC.

Summer 2016

*I*N LATE SUMMER of 2016, I landed at the Vancouver airport. It was another trip to visit with my parents. They pulled up to the airport in their Toyota Matrix, Dad behind the wheel, as usual. And on the ride back to Burnaby, Mom chatted excitedly, as usual.

"Did you eat on the plane?"

"How's the weather in Toronto?"

"Is the gas as expensive in Toronto?"

"What's Anthony doing in Toronto while you're gone?"

It was late, and I was tired, and I answered most of her questions half-heartedly. Plus, my mind was elsewhere. It was just a few months after Anthony and I had finished our cross-country road trip. During our travels, I'd seen my own parents in so many restaurant owners' faces. So many of the men and women I spoke with reminded me specifically of Dad.

The restaurant connection was a part of it. Until his retirement about ten years earlier, Dad worked in restaurants. The food was different—Dad made "Western" food. He had been head chef at a big, buffet-style restaurant in Vancouver called the Copper Kettle in the 1980s. There, he made giant roasts, baked hams and wobbly jellied fruit moulds. Later, he started his own catering company where he served up large banquets for weddings and fancy corporate parties. When he came home at night, he'd sometimes bring us leftovers from the cold-cut platters the size of car tires, creamy fettuccine alfredo, and lasagna with crispy, cheesy crusts. Sure, the food was different, but restaurants were restaurants.

Many of the Chinese restaurant owners I'd met had even looked like him. This was likely because most of them had come from the same region in southern China as Dad—the same cluster of small villages outside of Guangzhou known as Toisan. They had the same eyes that squinted at the corners when they smiled. The same high cheekbones.

As the restaurant owners had sat across from me telling me their stories, I had often thought about my dad, and how many of the questions I was asking these owners were ones I'd never thought to ask him.

There were so many gaps in what I knew: What was his life like back in China? How did he wind up in Canada at age twenty-four? And why did he come to Vancouver decades after his own parents?

• • • • • • •

Growing up, Dad was just "Dad." In the mornings, he'd drop us off at school in his Honda hatchback. And at night, he'd come home from work, scrape the dried tomato sauce or meat grease off his hands and then begin making our dinner. We'd eat quietly, heads hunched over, the sound of chewing only punctuated by chopsticks clicking against our bowls. Afterward, he'd watch the Cantonese medical dramas and cop shows they played on the Chinese-language channel until it was time for bed. Every day was the same.

On the weekends, when he wasn't working his second job as a contractor or his third job as a landscaper, he'd ferry us between lessons or attend our piano recitals and ballet performances. Sitting in his chair, his eyes closed, he'd nod along to the music in his paint-splattered polos.

He had a few hobbies. He liked to read. And sometimes he'd practise calligraphy, practising his brush strokes by writing classical Chinese poems. Later, he would also take up hiking and travelling. But when we were growing up, pretty much all of his time was spent working.

He did it all quietly. He didn't talk about himself. He definitely didn't talk much about his life before us. He seemed to prefer listening to talking.

The year I turned twenty-one, I left Vancouver and moved to Toronto with vague ideas of a career in journalism. He drove me to the airport. On the car ride there, he barely spoke a single word. And at the airport, he refused to help me lug my giant suitcases onto the baggage belt. "You're going to have to do things for yourself now," he said quietly but sternly. I know he just couldn't bear to do it himself.

After that, our conversations were limited to the brief phone calls I would make back to Vancouver—quick exchanges of

"Hi, how are you?" before passing the phone over to Mom. Visits home were crowded with other family and friends. On the rare occasion we were alone together, the conversation stayed focused on practical matters. He'd ask about the real estate market in Toronto. Or about the weather we'd been having. Or what I wanted to eat for dinner.

It seemed like a cliché. The stereotypical Asian dad, stoic and incapable of expressing his feelings. But that wasn't entirely true. The stereotype wouldn't explain how, when I was in kindergarten, he was the one to brush and style my hair each morning. It also wouldn't explain the time he was the only one who could make my cousin Taylor, then still an infant, stop crying by rocking her to sleep, curled up on his chest. Or the many lunches he packed for me during university, when he knew I was busy with studying. The sandwiches he rolled up into neat pinwheels. The carrots he carved into flowers.

The truth was, I hadn't spent much time getting to know him as an adult either. I had just treated him as "Dad."

But then we got the news.

For several months in the summer of 2015, doctors had been concerned about a tumour they'd found in Dad's liver. At the end of July—just a week before Anthony and I had our wedding in Montreal—the results of the biopsy confirmed the diagnosis. It was cholangiocarcinoma, or cancer of the bile duct. At the wedding, after Dad gave his father-of-the-bride toast, I clutched him and cried.

After the diagnosis, it was one piece of bad news after another, each more dire than the last. On our honeymoon, Anthony held my hands as I read the text from my sister: the cancer was inoperable. Most patients survived for just nine months. There was no hope of a cure.

Each time, we'd think, *How will we cope?* And eventually, we'd adjust. And then days later, there'd be another blow. Over and over again, until trauma began to feel normal.

"I feel fine," Dad would say. "As long as I can walk, as long as I can eat, I am okay." He'd go through one cycle of chemo and then the next.

For the first while, he really did seem fine. Between the chemo cycles, he still went on his Saturday hikes, leading his hiking group up countless trails, the bells he'd sewn onto his backpack to warn away bears jangling behind him. He still shopped at the supermarket and made dinner every Sunday.

"I'm not going anywhere anytime soon," he told us.

We all coped in our own ways. Mom fretted from one Chinese doctor to the next, bringing home bundles of herbs and roots she thought might heal him. Pansy kept track of his schedule, managing his dozens of appointments, tests and procedures, and making sure he knew how to prepare for each one. And Amber paid frequent visits, helping out around the house and plotting ways to get him out, even if it was just a walk in the park with her dog.

From Toronto, I awaited news. I pitched stories to my editors that would allow me to spend weeks or months at a time in Vancouver. But during these visits, I was at a loss for what to do. The day-to-day stuff—the ferrying-Dad-to-appointments, the organizing, the important stuff, my sisters and Mom already had covered.

I tried to find time alone with him. But he was still Dad. He wasn't interested in small talk, much less discussing what he was going through. I'd ask how he was, if there was anything he'd want to talk about, and he'd only shrug, as if to say, *Would it help?*

More often than not, we'd wind up sitting in silence—Dad watching TV, or slumped over in his chair, eyes closed, lost in thought.

• • • • • • •

As kids, we pretty much only saw Dad's parents Ye Ye and Ah Ngeen on holidays. There was always a stiffness to those visits, particularly between Dad and *his* dad, Ye Ye. I'd heard bits and pieces of arguments over the years. About that one time Mom and Dad went to visit with Pansy, then still an infant, and how Ye Ye wouldn't let them in the house. By the time I was a teenager, both grandparents had passed away. The day Ye Ye died, Dad started smoking again. He was moody for a long time. Withdrawn. Whatever the two of them had fought over, they'd never managed to resolve.

No one ever explained what had happened. All I had was what I had gathered through the years—overheard phone calls, the clenched whispers in the kitchen. And Dad didn't seem to want us to know. Gradually, I pieced together that it all seemed to stem from the same issue. It was the one thing we were never supposed to talk about: Dad had been left behind in China. His parents had come to Canada without him. It wasn't clear if he knew why. And if he did, he wasn't sharing.

Mom had freely shared her own stories over the years. While

Dad was cautious and careful, she was outspoken and emotional. Over dinner, or on long car rides between ballet and piano classes, she'd tell me about growing up in Hong Kong—about her father, Ah Ye, and how he'd dreamed of writing for newspapers but died when she was just nine. She'd lower her voice to just above a pained whisper as she described how Po Po had supported her and her three siblings by running a wonton shop in Hong Kong. And how she'd followed her brother, my Uncle Zachary, to Vancouver after he'd immigrated here in 1971.

But Dad had always kept his stories closely guarded. If someone mentioned Mao, Dad might let out a flash of anger. Or if they mentioned Pierre Trudeau, a burst of approval. Otherwise, he'd only shake his head on the rare occasion we'd think to ask. He'd slowly raise his arm, as if to say, *Stop.*

"*Duk la,*" he'd say, still shaking his head. Enough.

In the car, Dad kept driving silently. Mom had given up after my umpteenth vague response. She switched on the radio, which crackled the Chinese local news. In my head, an idea was bubbling.

"Dad, what are you doing tomorrow?"

His response came in a grunt. "Nothing," he said in Cantonese.

Perfect, I thought.

• • • • • • •

The next afternoon, as Dad was just settling in his favourite spot on the couch, next to the window, and curling in the sun, like a cat, I parked myself on the other couch beside him.

"I want to know about the Legion Cafe," I told him. It was a restaurant he'd owned with my mom, in the 1970s, before I was even born.

Growing up, I'd heard occasional mentions of the Legion. How Mom and Dad had moved out to Abbotsford, about an hour outside of Vancouver and at that point very much a small town. They had owned it for several years, then shut it down. It was one of two restaurants they had run in Abbotsford before eventually moving back to Vancouver. I'd heard a few anecdotes—Dad's offhand comments about learning to make chicken à la king at the Legion, and laughing about how many hours they'd put in for so little money. But I knew little about the restaurant. I'd seen a picture before—a sepia-toned image of a restaurant counter, with a soda fountain and a "soup of the day" board. Chicken soup and tuna sandwiches. But I didn't understand how that restaurant fit in with his later life in Vancouver.

Maybe if I started asking him about food and his restaurants, just as I had in my many interviews on the cross-country trip, I could get him talking about other things too.

"Why Abbotsford?" I asked.

"How did you learn to cook the food?"

"Is that where you learned to cook?"

At first, he shrugged off my questions. He ignored them, then pretended he was taking a nap. But when it became clear I wasn't giving up, and that I wouldn't let him watch his TV show in peace, he let out a long sigh. He stood up and wandered toward the front room of the house. A few moments later, he returned with a dark brown binder. Holding his reading glasses in his hand, he crouched down on the floor over the binder.

I had seen that brown binder hundreds of times before. It had always been there, sitting on the bookshelf in the room we called "the piano room" because of the grand piano we had always complained about having to practise on—the piano that Dad worked three jobs and my mom the night shift to pay for.

I crouched down on the floor next to him. This binder, he explained, was how he learned how to cook "Western" food. Before working in his first kitchen, he told me, he'd had no idea what a lasagna was. He could barely pronounce the word. Nor did he know how to properly truss a chicken, or what turkey "dressing" meant. He'd relied on this binder and his collection of cookbooks to figure it out.

Flipping through the pages, he showed me sheet after sheet of plain white paper. On them, he'd carefully recorded in his neat, all-caps handwriting the recipes he'd learned over the years. "Quiche Lorraine." "Chicken Liver Pate." "Cream Puffs." He could have written the recipes in Chinese, but he wanted to do them in English, to do it "properly." So there was "Pazza Sauce" with "Mints" (mince). And "Cream Dip" with notes such as: "Can make in to crab. Shrimp or what ev." He'd learned by watching his colleagues, or tearing recipes out of magazines. Every time he saw something he liked, he put it in the binder.

"I think it's in here somewhere," he mumbled in Cantonese as he thumbed through the pages.

His eyes scanned down page after page. Occasionally he

would say something under his breath, then flip to the next page.

Finally, he stopped on a page, taking a long moment to read it.

"I only have the second page," he said finally. He handed it to me, a thick sheet of greying paper. The text was typed out with a typewriter. It was the menu from the Legion.

"COMBINATION SPECIAL," it said in all-caps letters across the top. The rest was organized into a grid. There was a "Dinner for 2," "Dinner for 4" and so on.

I scanned the page up and down, trying to make sense of it. "What is this?"

"The Legion," he said. "You asked about the Legion."

I scanned it again, reading it more carefully this time.

There was no chicken soup on this menu. No turkey sandwiches or BLTs.

My eyes focused instead on two words that repeated themselves over and over across the page: "chop suey."

"Dinner for 2" included chicken chop suey.

"Dinner for 4" had beef chop suey.

"Dinner for 6" had vegetarian chop suey.

I studied the rest of the page. There was chicken chow mein, egg rolls and sweet and sour pork.

I blinked hard, then turned the sheet over. There it was, in all-caps letters across the top. "CHINESE FOODS."

I looked at Dad, still sitting across from me crouched over the binder.

"Dad."

He looked up.

"The Legion Cafe—it was a *Chinese* restaurant?"

He scrunched his face. "It was mixed. It was a mixed restaurant," he said.

I was stunned. Never before had I heard about the Legion serving Chinese food. Never before had I known my parents had run a Chinese restaurant. All those years growing up, my dad would turn up his nose at chop suey–type Chinese restaurants. "This is fake Chinese," he would say. Even when I'd gone on my cross-country road trip, he had seemed puzzled that I should travel all that way just to write about chop suey restaurants. Neither he nor Mom had mentioned that they'd owned one.

I shook my head slowly, back and forth, trying to gather my thoughts. "Why didn't you guys say anything?"

Dad looked back at me and shrugged. "I thought you knew."

A few moments later, he added, "Actually, we had two."

Two Chinese restaurants. He kept talking, but I was no longer focusing on what he was saying. All I could think was this: just months earlier, I had travelled over nine thousand kilometres, through snow and sleet. For eighteen days, I had lived out of a suitcase, driving from one small town to the next, interviewing all those Chinese families. All of it to learn the stories behind Chinese restaurants. To each of the families, I had asked the same question, over and over: "How did you wind up in this place?"

All the while, I had barely managed to scratch the surface of my own family's story.

That was when I realized my journey wasn't yet over.

Vulcan, AB.

Spring 2016

O N THE THIRD night of our trip, Anthony and I had dinner with my family at a Malaysian-Chinese restaurant in East Vancouver. The restaurant was an unfussy spot, with walls painted green and televisions mounted to the walls. My sisters, Anthony and I chatted about our trip so far, about our two days in Victoria, and our plan to drive west for eleven hours straight the next day. Meanwhile, Mom and Dad studied the menu.

I overheard pieces of their conversation. They were trying to decide which dishes were most economical.

"The rice is on special."

"This one comes in a huge plate."

A few moments later, they landed on the Hainanese chicken—whole poached chicken with rice cooked in pandan leaves. It would taste just as good as leftovers with rice the next day.

When the waitress came over, Mom and Dad ordered for us all: *char kway teow*, *roti canai*, Hainanese chicken, satay chicken skewers and steaming bowls of *laksa*. Soon, our table began to pile up with dishes. Smoky, pan-fried rice noodles, flaky fried flatbreads we dipped into golden curry sauce and ate with our hands, and noodles swimming in coconut curry broth. Dinner in Vancouver with my parents almost always meant Chinese. Still, that almost always meant something different.

The 1980s and 1990s introduced Canada to a new kind of Chinese. Unlike the previous waves of mainly poor, rural Chinese, now there were hundreds of thousands of middle-class and wealthy Hong Kongers fleeing to Vancouver and Toronto ahead of the looming 1997 China handover.

This group included some of Hong Kong's most highly skilled, highly trained Cantonese chefs. These chefs, together with the affluent newcomers, propelled a boom of excellent Cantonese restaurants in the cities—places where glimmering rock cod and spiny king crab were scooped live out of squeaky-clean tanks (not like the cloudy-water Chinatown places), steamed expertly and served over pressed white tablecloths.

This was the Vancouver I grew up in. After we moved to Burnaby when I was in high school, it was as common to hear Cantonese or Taiwanese in our cafeteria as English. Many of my classmates were "CBCs" like me—Canadian-born Chinese whose parents had come from the poor areas of southern China decades earlier. But many others were newcomers and so-called "satellite kids." Their parents set them up with brand-new houses and cars, then returned to Taiwan or Hong Kong for work. The student parking lot was filled with BMWs and Mercedes, in stark contrast to the Toyotas and Chryslers in the teachers' lot.

The sudden arrival of these new Chinese resulted in tensions, just as they had a century ago. These newcomers weren't content settling in the East Vancouver areas around Chinatown, or working-class south Vancouver. Some of them bought homes in the city's toniest neighbourhoods, traditionally white areas like Kerrisdale and Shaughnessy. When they immigrated, some tore down the existing homes, building new ones in their place. They wanted the types of homes they could never have back in crowded Hong Kong—brand-new houses with lots of space.

This led to some ugly stand-offs—racial tensions disguised as complaints about so-called "monster homes." The concerns, according to some local residents at the time, had nothing to do with race. They had to do with real estate and heritage preservation, with the character of the homes, the trees and *bad taste.*

But the subtext was just barely below the surface. "The face of Vancouver is changing far too quickly," said one letter written to a Vancouver city councillor at the time. "We—the fairly reasonable people—fear the power that the Hong Kong money wields. We resent the fact that because they come here with pats of money they are able to mutilate the areas they choose to settle in," she wrote. "These people come—with no concern for our past."

More recently, the influx of Chinese newcomers has been from mainland China. This included some of the hyper-wealthy *fu er dai,* a new class of Chinese—the children of China's nouveau riche. These *new* new Chinese have faced their own backlash, especially the wealthiest ones. Again, the tensions have been framed around housing, with many locals blaming the wealthy Chinese for skyrocketing real estate prices.

But in fact the *new* newcomers are a diverse set, including middle-class and poor Chinese too. They arrived in Vancouver from all China's many cities and regions. Suddenly Mandarin took over from Cantonese as the most-spoken Chinese language in Vancouver, and it became as common to hear Fujianese as Cantonese in Toronto's restaurant kitchens. These newcomers brought with them to Canada great, authentic and diverse regional Chinese cuisines. No longer was it only Cantonese or "chop suey" Chinese. In the past two decades, the strip plazas along Highway 7 in Markham, or along Alexandra Road in Richmond, have suddenly seen all kinds of new restaurants popping up, offering lamb cumin burgers and *liang pi*, the cold, sesame and chili-drenched wheat noodles I love from the Shanxi province. Or paper-thin *xiao long bao,* soup dumplings as good as the ones in Shanghai (or so I've been told). China-based chains, such as QJD Peking Duck or Dagu Rice Noodle, have opened up Canadian locations too. These companies have an almost entirely Chinese clientele and don't feel the need to cater to "Western" tastes.

At the same time, next-generation Chinese chefs—those who grew up in Canada like me—were opening restaurants with their own spin on Chinese. Patois in Toronto tells the story of the Chinese who immigrated elsewhere, in this case, Jamaica, before coming to Canada with dishes like "dirty fried rice" with *lap cheong* and the "Cajun trinity" of bell peppers, celery and onion. At DaiLo in Toronto, chef Nick Liu riffs off his Hakkanese ancestry with dishes such as pumpkin dumplings with soy brown butter sauce and truffles. That dish is topped with a glaze of White Rabbit candies, the milky, chewy candy ubiquitous in every Chinese household. It's a dish that reminds me of childhood visits with Po Po, who used to press the little white candies into my palms with a knowing glance. *Our little secret*, that glance seemed to say.

In another time, this cuisine might have been described as inauthentic, or worse, dismissed as the f-word, "fusion." But for these chefs, the cuisine is authentic to their own experiences.

Still, these cultural mash-ups were a cuisine my dad could never quite understand. "This isn't *mapo tofu*," he said once, grimacing, after I cooked him the classic Sichuan dish. As a Christmas gift, my sisters had gotten me *The Mission Chinese Food Cookbook* by the Korean-born, Oklahoma-raised chef Danny Bowien, and Chris Ying, and I had been excited to start cooking from it. The *mapo tofu* was mostly classic, with lots of *doubanjiang* and Sichuan peppercorns. But the sauce was rounded out with a couple teaspoons of tomato paste and liberal heapings of "angry lady" chili sauce. To my dad, at least on that day, the deviations were a mistake. Authenticity, he seemed to argue, was critical. He knew what it was like before we could find authentic *mapo tofu* in Vancouver. What it was like before the rest of Canada knew to appreciate it.

Yet here we were now, eating our *roti canai* and *laksa*, created by Chinese immigrants in southeast Asia. After the Chinese began settling in places like Malaysia, they added local ingredients and traditions—such as coconut milk, coriander, cumin and turmeric—into Chinese noodle soup dishes. A new cuisine was born. It was never authentically Chinese, but over time it did become authentically Malaysian.

And in that moment, as we slurped the noodles swimming in the golden coconut broth, none of that mattered anyway. All that mattered was that the dish was delicious.

. . . .

About two hours after Anthony and I left Vancouver, it began to snow. In my planning, I had neglected to consider snow as a possibility, so accustomed had I become to Ontario's generally warm spring weather. I huddled gratefully into my winter coat.

As we climbed north on the Coquihalla Highway in our impossibly tiny car, big fat snowflakes floated down from the sky, dancing on the windshield before disappearing. In the distance, grey-blue mountains with snow-capped peaks came into focus.

We climbed higher and higher, the road slowly disappearing under the drift.

It was a lovely scene, except for the signs that began to appear along the highway.

"MUST USE WINTER TIRES," one warned in thick black letters.

I turned and looked at Anthony. "Hey, do we have winter tires?"

He blinked. "They're all-season."

I didn't know a lot about cars, but I did know enough to understand those weren't the same thing. But I kept quiet.

A few moments later he said, rather unwisely, "As long as we don't run out of gas, we'll be fine." The signs warned that the next gas station was at least 150 kilometres away.

He must have sensed my tension, because he added, quickly, "We're fine."

This was a usual routine for us. I would worry. He would reassure. And his apparent lack of concern would cause me to worry even more.

We climbed higher up the mountain, the signs growing increasingly alarming.

"Steep grade ahead."

"Expect sudden weather changes."

In my head, I was beginning to run through the worst possible scenario of getting snowed in.

What kind of clothes were packed in our suitcases? Were they warm enough if we were left stranded on the highway overnight?

Would the stuff we had in the car—a giant jug of water and a couple of juice boxes—last us until the morning?

Was my phone still getting reception?

After a while, the signs were in all-caps lettering, screaming out for our attention. They simply read: "BE CAUTIOUS."

"Anthony," I said, giving him a hard look.

He turned to look at me, taking in my expression.

All I could think of was the girl at the rental office and her alarmed reaction. But just as he was about to speak, I realized my ears were popping. We looked out our windows to see that the car wasn't tilting upward anymore. We were done climbing. We had peaked, and the worst was behind us.

I exhaled a long, slow breath.

From the driver's seat, Anthony shrugged. "See?" he said in a way that he likely thought was calming, but I instead found infuriating. "I told you we'd be fine."

• • • • • • •

The next morning we drove south, away from our hotel in Calgary and into a haze of blue sky and golden wheat fields. The entire highway seemed bathed in sun.

About an hour outside the city, we spotted the first telltale clue of an upcoming Prairie town: a dingy-looking grain elevator, the only structure interrupting an otherwise unbroken horizon. Then, a gas station, a house or two along the side of the highway, and a giant warehouse selling John Deere tractors and farm equipment. And then the welcome sign. At each of the Prairie towns, there was always a sign, welcoming us to Vegreville, or Grenfell, or Boissevain. At the bottom of the sign, hanging off two rusty hooks, a placard would boast of whichever NHL player happened to have grown up in the tiny town. Each time, Anthony would nod knowingly.

This sign looked a little different. It was made of concrete and scripted in a futuristic-looking font.

"Welcome to Vulcan," it said.

The town itself looked different too. Right beside the sign was a giant floating saucer—a white spaceship hoisted into the air on a pedestal. And right next to *it* was a space station of sorts, a building painted all white with circular windows, a domed roof and a satellite reaching up into the sky.

"A space station?" I said aloud.

Anthony quickly corrected me. "Not a space station," he said. "A Trek station."

I glanced over at him. He was trying to act cool, but I could see a grin spreading across his face. He slowed the car down to barely a crawl in order to take everything in. I'd seen the DVD collection he'd amassed over the years, including multiple *Star Trek* boxed sets. I'd also seen how defensive he got whenever I referred to him as a Trekkie. But now we were in Vulcan, in the heartland of *Star Trek* fandom. His glee was impossible to conceal.

Of the towns on the CP Railway in the early twentieth century, Vulcan had the highest elevation, and railway surveyors assumed it would be the most prosperous. So they named it Vulcan, after the Roman god of fire. For a time, the name was well-suited. The town's strategic location—amid fields of wheat and barley, and right on the railway line—made it a hub for the wheat industry. For decades, the town was surrounded by rows of giant wooden elevators. But by the 1980s those elevators began shutting down one by one. The large grain companies replaced them with newer, more efficient designs elsewhere.

With the economy struggling, the town looked around for new opportunities. By then, *Star Trek* had become wildly popular, and by coincidence the name "Vulcan" had a special significance on the show. Already, officials had noticed some curious tourists making trips to their town because of it. *Star Trek,* they thought, might be their opportunity. So all of Vulcan became involved, painting *Star Trek* murals on street corners, starting *Star Trek* museums and over time building a town-sized shrine to the television show.

I realized I had no idea what "Vulcans" even were.

"Vulcans are a species, and the place where they're from—a planet," Anthony said, explaining as he drove, taking us farther into town. "It's where Spock was from."

I was still confused.

He rolled his eyes and added, "Pointy ears."

"Oh, *those*."

We drove slowly down Centre Street, past gas stations and parking lots. There was a Legion on the right, just before the railroad tracks, and temporary-looking buildings separated by large parking lots. There was a liquor store, a Home Hardware and neat-looking homes with vinyl sidings.

But every few blocks, there would be another reminder of the TV show. A giant mural on the side of a hair salon. A *Star Trek* museum, where we would later pop in to find a lone employee guiding a small tour group through a room filled with costumes and memorabilia (the museum has since closed and moved to Drumheller). And at one street corner, in front of a set of hedges, a bronze bust of Leonard Nimoy dressed as Spock. It was a memorial from the time the actor paid a visit to the small town. Beneath it was his handprint pressed into bronze, fingers spread in the "Vulcan salute."

Every few minutes, Anthony stopped to take a photo. "What?" he said sheepishly when he caught me smirking. "I just want to send the pictures to my friends."

Finally, we found ourselves in front of the New Club Café. This was the real reason we were here. I wanted to see what a Chinese restaurant (that, according to Google, sold both chop suey and pizza) looked like in the middle of this *Trek*-obsessed town. But as we moved closer, my heart sank. The lights were off. There was a "Closed" sign at the door. A bucket and mop sat abandoned near the entryway.

I looked at Anthony, who grimaced. "Too bad," he said. He looked genuinely sad. "It looks so cool too," he said in a quiet voice. It did. The sign had a retro look to it. On the left was the restaurant's name and logo, printed in blue and red. And on the right, in thick yellow lettering, just two words: "STEAK" and "PIZZA."

I knocked on the door, pressing my face up to the smeared glass in case there was someone in the back. No one answered.

We paused there for a few moments, figuring out what to do. "Do you want to go to the next town?"

I sighed. I'd had high hopes for the New Club Café. I had developed a long list of restaurants along our route weeks ago. Because we were travelling by car and didn't yet know when we'd be arriving in each town, I hadn't called most of them ahead of time. I'd wanted to be flexible. But the downside was that I didn't always have a backup plan. A few doors down, another restaurant caught my eye. So I suggested we get some coffee and regroup there.

As soon as we walked in, the waitress, a younger woman with dark hair and an easy smile, showed us to a table. As we waited, I thumbed my phone, trying to figure out whether there were other towns and restaurants nearby that might be worth trying. The waitress returned to take our order and I couldn't help but ask, "Do you happen to know the owners of the New Club Café?"

She shook her head but seemed curious. I explained why we were there.

"Well, you can always just go to the other Chinese restaurant," she said after a moment.

Other Chinese restaurant? The population of the entire town was around 1,700, roughly the number of students at my high school back in Vancouver. The fact that it had even one Chinese restaurant had surprised me. Now she was telling me there were two?

She smiled and pointed back in the direction of the highway. "It's called Amy's," she said. "The owners just moved here not too long ago from China."

"I'm not an expert," she said, shooting me a nervous glance. "But it seems, you know—authentic."

• • • • • • •

It turned out we'd passed Amy's on our way into town, not even noticing it. And no wonder. The restaurant was on a service road just off the highway and next to a gas station. It was built with red brick, with a familiar pavilion-style roof. I suspected the building may have lived a previous life as a pizza restaurant. The green sign said, "Amy's—Family Restaurant." There was no mention of Chinese food.

I pulled open the glass door to find a large dining room with wooden chairs and dark green tables. Country music was playing from the speakers. A group of seniors sat around a large table having their lunch, their walkers just a few feet away. On the other side of the dining room, a middle-aged couple—a woman with glasses and a man in a flannel shirt—sat with plates heaped with spring rolls, and beef with broccoli.

In the centre of the room was a long buffet table with heat lamps hanging from the top. Chafing dishes were filled with perfectly round golden chicken balls, bright green pieces of broccoli stir-fried with thinly sliced carrots, and crispy-looking meat coated in deep-fried batter. All of it glistening under the light. At a separate, shorter buffet table were desserts, quivering cubes of red Jell-O and pre-cut squares of cake.

A Chinese teenager, about fifteen, walked toward us. He seemed startled when he took me in. A few of the seniors eyed me quizzically too. I guessed from their reactions that the restaurant didn't see many Chinese customers.

The teenager seated us in the far room, near the middle-aged couple, then left us alone with the buffet.

By then, it was around noon, so we approached it greedily. Anthony piled his plate high with chow mein, fried rice and a few onion rings. From across the buffet table, he grinned happily. This was what he'd been waiting for. He's not Chinese. And, as much as he was always game to trek out to whatever latest Shanxi-style noodle shop or Taiwanese hot pot restaurant I became obsessed with through the years, the chicken-ball-and-fried-rice Chinese still held a special place in his heart. This was the Chinese food he grew up with. It was what he still craved from time to time, turning to me every few months to say, "Can we go get some *good* fake Chinese?"

I circled the buffet table carefully, choosing just a few items—some broccoli, a small tangle of chow mein and a couple strips of fried fish. We still had over a week and a half of travel ahead of us, and likely dozens of Chinese restaurants to visit. I wanted to pace myself. We sat down and dug in. The broccoli was perfectly cooked, still crunchy and bright green. The chow mein had been fried in a fiery-hot wok, and had *wok hay*. The noodles had been cooked properly, with a fiery-hot wok and the perfect amount of oil, so they neither stuck together nor dripped with grease. And though the fish had likely come from frozen, the strips were crispy and hot, fresh from the fryer. This was the good "fake Chinese" Anthony was always asking for.

When my plate was almost empty, I spotted the teenage server across the room and signalled to him. I asked if the restaurant's owner was around. He looked puzzled, but nodded and disappeared behind a door. A few minutes later, a young woman with glasses and long, straight hair pulled back into a ponytail approached our table. She looked no older than thirty and had smooth, pale skin. She introduced herself as the manager.

"You're the owner?"

"Yes," she said. Her English was clear but hesitant, so I switched to Mandarin, the language of most Mainland Chinese, and one I've learned through the years but am far from fluent in.

"You're from Beijing?" It was a guess, based on her accent.

"*Bu shi,*" she said. No. She introduced herself as Qin Lin and told me she was from Guangdong.

She sat up tall in her chair as she spoke. Each time I asked her a question, she paused thoughtfully before answering. She had a polite, easy manner, the air of the star pupil in school, bright and eager to help. As we spoke, Anthony kept eating, oblivious to what we were talking about. Not that he seemed to mind. He had gone back for seconds when we first started talking.

Back in China, Ms. Lin's job had been to print logos on T-shirts, she said. From morning to night, she worked in the Guangdong factory, her husband working alongside her. At the end of each day, the shirts would be packed in plastic and shipped in boxes to countries all over the world. They would go home. And the next morning, they'd arrive back at the factory to start their work all over again.

But then she had Cindy, her daughter. No longer were they just thinking about their own lives and their own futures. They had her future to think about too.

Ms. Lin had originally grown up in Kaiping, a county near Toisan. Like Toisan, Kaiping was one of the *siyup* counties, or "four counties." It was an especially poverty-stricken area in southern China near Guangzhou that, during decades of drought, flooding and famine, was slowly drained of almost all of its young people. Most of them went overseas, eventually sending money back to their hometowns.

Ms. Lin's husband had an aunt who had gone to Canada, to a city called Winnipeg. She offered to help settle them there. Ms. Lin and her husband did the mental calculation. They were two factory workers with little education. Their fates had already been decided in China. And to Ms. Lin, that meant Cindy's too. In China, Ms. Lin said, "It's all about *guan xi*"—relationships and family connections.

In Canada, the aunt had told them, Cindy would start with a clean slate. It didn't matter that her parents were factory workers, or that they had been born in rural villages. If Cindy studied hard and did well, she could have the same opportunities as everyone else.

They weighed that against what they would give up in Guangdong: their friends, their families—all of their comforts and everything they knew. Still, the decision seemed obvious.

It was Christmas day when they arrived in Winnipeg. It was cold and the city felt dirty. Their aunt came to pick them up from the airport, whisking them past flashing lights and signs they couldn't understand.

• • • • • • •

Sitting across from me, Ms. Lin glanced at Cindy. The little girl, now eleven, was sitting at the table next to us, pretending to draw. Every few moments, she snuck glances at us from behind the backrest of her chair. A few times, she wandered over to our table, listening to parts of our conversation.

Almost five years had passed since that day at the Winnipeg airport. Ms. Lin and her husband had spent the first three years in Winnipeg learning English and working various odd jobs, she in the factory that builds Greyhound buses and he in the local EQ3 warehouse assembling furniture.

Then one of his cousins asked if they wanted to take over the lease at a Chinese restaurant she was running in a town called Vulcan. Initially Ms. Lin was scared. She had grown accustomed to Winnipeg. She liked her English teacher and had begun making friends and starting a life in the city. She and her husband had figured out where to buy their Chinese vegetables and other groceries. Neither had ever heard of this town called Vulcan. But this was another opportunity. Instead of working in factories, they could work for themselves.

So they moved. Now, they'd been here for two years. "It's quiet here, but it's very nice," Ms. Lin said in Mandarin. They were just two years into the ten-year lease, but she wasn't yet sure if the family would stay permanently in Vulcan. Business had been good at first, but then things slowed down. They'd had to lay off their one waitress and were now running everything themselves, with the occasional help of their nephew, the teenaged server.

She looked around the dining room at the dark green carpet and the heavy wood chairs. The work was hard, she said. Most days, they started at eight in the morning and kept working until midnight. Her husband was in the kitchen, and she took care of the dining room. When Cindy wasn't in school, she often spent her days in the restaurant. It was a gruelling schedule.

If they stayed here for the full ten years, Ms. Lin said, she hoped they might eventually buy a house. Cindy, she said, would study hard and go to a good university. Then she would get a good job—far, far away from dirty factory work or long, exhausting hours in a hot, smelly restaurant. Cindy, she hoped, would work in an office with heat in the winters and air conditioning in the summers. She'd have steady hours and good pay.

Ms. Lin switched to English. "A good job," she said. "Not like me."

The couple sitting near us signalled for the cheque, and Ms. Lin excused herself and walked out toward them.

With her mother gone, Cindy once again peered at me. She gave me a smile, and I smiled back at her.

A few minutes later, the couple stood up to leave.

It seemed like it was time for us to leave too, so we made our way toward the cash register to pay and thank Ms. Lin for her time. From that vantage point—Ms. Lin's perch near the entrance—there was a clear view across the highway of the Trek Station. Sitting inside Amy's, and talking with Ms. Lin, I had almost forgotten where we were.

Anthony couldn't help himself. "What do you think of all the *Star Trek* stuff?" he asked her.

We studied the white building, with its oddly shaped curves and circular windows.

But when we turned back at Ms. Lin, she was staring blankly at us. She seemed to have no idea what Anthony was talking about. I recalled Ms. Lin telling me, "All day, from morning to night, we work." It suddenly dawned on me that, with all her time spent in the restaurant, she had never noticed or paid any mind to the town's eccentricities. It may as well be any town. Work was work was work.

She stared back at us and repeated the English words, letting them roll off her tongue slowly: "*Star Trek?*"

Jingweicun, Guangdong, China.

1924–52

"HOW DO YOU say it?" I asked Dad over and over, making him repeat the name. We were both leaned over the kitchen table, peering at my laptop.

The first character in the name of the village wasn't a common Chinese word, and as such didn't have an obviously romanized spelling. For several minutes, I guessed, googling variations that made sense.

J-i-a-n-g

Z-e-n-g

Z-h-e-n-g

When that yielded no results, we decided to just try to find it on the map. He stood over my shoulder while I studied a map of southern China, telling me to move my cursor up or down, zoom in and out.

He read out the names of cities and regions as we scrolled past them. "Zhongshan, Jiangmen—a little bit more," he said.

"Toisan!" he called out triumphantly. The county he was from. "Okay, almost."

I zoomed in on an area labelled "Shuibuzhen" on the map. Dozens of little villages appeared on my screen, with two main highways cutting through them.

"Jingweicun! There!" He was excited now, pointing at the screen.

He couldn't believe his tiny village was on this map. He called out to Mom in the next room. "Frances! Hey Frances! Look, you can see Jingweicun on this!"

I zoomed in farther and farther, as close as I could get, and switched the map to satellite view.

The village was in fact just a few clusters of homes, spread out over large swaths of rural land parcels. He asked me to zoom in on each cluster, but furrowed his brow at each one.

"This could be it—no. Maybe this one—no."

He was trying to find his old house but couldn't. He'd been back to Guangdong and Jingweicun many times in recent years. He had seen firsthand much of the change that had happened in his old village—new developments filled with brand-new houses just down the street from the old dirt houses where he'd grown up.

He kept searching, mumbling under his breath, and I took in the image in front of me. It was fuzzy, just a haze of grainy greens and greys. There wasn't much there other than farmland, a few shacks and dirt roads.

"This is where you lived?" I asked my dad.

He nodded.

"This is where Ye Ye lived?"

He nodded again.

"And this is where his dad lived too?"

"They all lived there," he said. "As far as I know, all of our ancestors lived in Jingweicun."

I turned the image over and over in my head. It was just a tiny speck on the map, a few dirt roads, a jumble of ramshackle homes built of mud, all of it surrounded by rice paddies. This was where we were from. So how had we wound up here?

• • • • • • •

For the first two decades of Ye Ye's life, Jingweicun was his entire world, Dad told me.

Like most of the kids growing up in the village, Ye Ye was allowed a few years of schooling. But by about age ten, he was expected to work just like everyone else. And like everyone else in the village, and every one of his relatives before him, that work meant farming.

His first job was watching the pigs. Near the house was a rickety hut in which one of the neighbours kept his pigs. It was Ye Ye's job to care for them. From morning to night, he'd haul water back and forth, with the buckets propped up on his shoulders. At night, he and Bak Bak, his mother, would eat alone in their hut.

Much of the time, Ah Gong, Ye Ye's father, was gone. "Away" was all Ye Ye knew about where his dad had gone. One neighbour told him Ah Gong was working in Singapore. Another said Indonesia. Yet another said Holland. To Ye Ye, it hardly mattered. Away was away. Every few years, Ah Gong would resurface. He'd stay awhile with Ye Ye and Bak Bak and tell stories of his time abroad working as a carpenter—the buildings he'd built, and the entryways he'd carved out of wood. He'd talk about the friends he'd made and the sights he'd seen.

Once in a while, Ye Ye would hear the words "Gold Mountain." That's where Ah Gong had gone. It was what the neighbours told him too: "He's gone to *Gum San*."

Gum San. Gold Mountain. Ye Ye tried to imagine this place, a land paved with gold.

Other villagers had sons, nephews and other relatives who had also gone to Gold Mountain. The men in neighbouring villages had gone to Gold Mountain too. Over the course of decades, tens of thousands of young men had left this tiny part of China for Gold Mountain. These four *siyup* counties were so poor that the villages could only feed their sons by sending them away. Some villages were so poor they sent away all their young men. Gum San wasn't just one place. It could be Canada, or the United States, or Australia, or Holland. It just meant "away."

The few who returned to their villages came back with unimaginable luxuries, like Singer sewing machines, jackets and brand-new clothing. They brought back money to build houses and schools and parks. Those are the ones people called "Gold Mountain men." The young men in the villages would eye these men with envy. They wanted one day to be Gold Mountain men too.

But how could Ah Gong be a Gold Mountain man, Ye Ye wondered. He would leave for years at a time, each time coming back with just a few coins in his pocket. The other

Gold Mountain men sent money back to their families. They sent letters with enough money in them to support their wives and children in Jingweicun. But the envelopes from Ah Gong contained nothing but letters. Each time he returned to Jingweicun, he came back with less than when he'd left.

"*Ah-peen*," other relatives would later tell me, in a lowered voice. Opium. That was the reason Ah Gong never had anything to send back. He'd spent all his money on drugs.

So Bak Bak and Ye Ye were on their own. It was up to Ye Ye to support the family. They worked each day on their farms. Most days, they had enough to eat.

• • • • • • •

One day in 1949, when Ye Ye was twenty-five, Bak Bak went to meet with the village matchmaker. It was time for Ye Ye to marry. The matchmaker suggested a young woman from a neighbouring village. Her parents were farmers too.

At the matchmaker's house, Ye Ye saw her for the first time. She was eighteen, with straight black hair and a wide face. Ah Ngeen. They shared a pot of tea, sitting awkwardly on each side of a table while the relatives watched. Soon after, they were married. And less than a year later, in 1951, Dad was born.

That's when the letter arrived.

It was from Ye Ye's "great aunt." Whether she was really an aunt, or any kind of blood relation, no one seems to be sure, but she was from Jingweicun so it was all the same anyhow. She had left many years earlier and now owned her own farm in Canada.

She was looking for another worker on her farm, she wrote. Ye Ye could go work for her if he wanted. She was offering him the chance to go to Gold Mountain.

It was around here where Dad's retelling began to grow fuzzy. There were gaps he was missing. Questions he couldn't—or wouldn't—answer.

"What exactly was the offer?" I asked.

"Why him?"

"Did he understand what he was getting into?"

"Why would he leave then, when his son had only just been born?"

But Dad only shrugged. "It was a long time ago," he said.

I couldn't tell if he genuinely didn't know or if he was being intentionally vague. Either way, it seemed there was much more to the story.

He didn't tell me what else was in that letter. All he told me was this: Ye Ye's answer to the great aunt's letter was yes.

Soon after, he boarded an airplane and left Jingweicun for Canada.

He went alone.

Drumheller, AB.

Spring 2016

*A*BOUT AN HOUR and a half after leaving Vulcan, we reached the Canadian Badlands. Surrounding us in every direction were rocky canyons. Thousands of years of erosion revealed clay-coloured stripes. According to the signs, coal and dinosaur bones had been discovered here going back to the nineteenth century.

Anthony squinted as he drove, taking it all in. "Can you imagine settling in this place?" he said. As a history buff, he'd always been fascinated by the Prairies and by the pioneers who first headed west to build this "western front." The Ukrainians and Poles came in large groups, lured by promises of cheap land and a new beginning.

We took in the gnarled rock formations off in the distance.

A few minutes later, we saw the town signs for Drumheller. Like Vulcan, this town had found its own brand to draw tourists. In this case, it was dinosaurs. Drumheller's welcome sign was concrete, with the town name engraved in thick block letters and flanked by a *Tyrannosaurus rex*. Capitalizing on the dinosaur bone discoveries in the Badlands, Drumheller now calls itself the "dinosaur capital of the world." We drove through the town, taking in the dinosaur figurines that greeted passersby from street corners, park benches and bus stops.

Hovering over the entire town was a giant green *Tyrannosaurus rex*, twenty-five metres tall. We climbed the staircase built into the spine of the T. rex, up into the observation deck built into its jaw. Looking out, the town sprawled in front of us, with tidy-looking parks and homes, and the Badlands in the distance.

Back in the car, we drove down Centre Street, passing a seniors' centre and a thrift shop. The town had the nostalgic feel of a summer town from the 1970s, with faded gift shops, laser tag and a small movie theatre. But as we made our way around, I realized the only other cars we had seen were the ones parked in the parking lots. Some of the storefronts appeared shuttered. And there wasn't a single person walking on the sidewalks. It was a town of about six and a half thousand— large enough for its own Wal-Mart and McDonald's—but its town centre felt even quieter than Vulcan's.

We parked in front of Diana Restaurant on Centre Street. Sandwiched between an Econo Lodge and a salon, the restaurant didn't look like much. It was housed in a plain beige-brick building that could have been a dentist or medical supply office. But inside, it was like a 1960s film set that had since gone untouched. This was the glamorous Chinese restaurant from Hollywood movies, all dim lighting, wood carvings and beaded curtains. The walls were covered with heavy, brocaded wallpaper and Chinese watercolours. The banquettes were bright red and plastic. Paper dragons with golden beards and long red tails hung from the ceiling. An empty buffet table sat abandoned in the corner.

By that time, it was mid-afternoon and the restaurant was near-empty. We'd already had lunch back in Vulcan and were too full for a second meal. But I still wanted to order something. Behind the counter, I spotted a poster advertising bubble tea. Perfect.

A woman who looked to be in her thirties, with short, neat hair, approached. I ordered a taro bubble tea to go. She nodded, then disappeared into the back. A few minutes later, she returned with my drink.

"You're the owner here?" I asked her in Mandarin.

She nodded quietly. She was shy but seemed intrigued when I explained why I was asking.

We chatted politely for a few minutes as I sipped my drink. I'd chosen quickly, defaulting to taro flavour only because it had been my favourite as a teenager. When made fresh from the root and mixed with milk, taro becomes sweet and fragrant. But the drink I'd been handed was clearly made from a powder. It was sweet and dessert-like, but dense and chalky.

Her name was Linda Xie, she said. In China, she had worked as an accountant. She was quiet and reserved, and seemed like she'd be happy sitting behind a desk crunching numbers. She and her husband, Peter Li, had come to Drumheller ten years earlier, from Datong, a city in Shanxi province in China. Peter's uncle was already running a restaurant in Drumheller, and offered to sponsor them.

A few minutes later, a man with a Buddha-like face and build walked into the restaurant. It was Peter. At first he was puzzled to see the two of us sitting there, but as soon as he heard my (very poor) Mandarin, his face quickly gave way to a puckish grin. Unlike Ms. Xie, Mr. Li was boisterous and outspoken.

He sat down with us, leaning back against the seat like he could sit all day. "What do you want to know?" he asked. "I'm happy to tell you everything."

Ms. Xie, who had dutifully put up with my questions, seemed grateful for his arrival. She quickly stood up and excused herself.

There was only one table that was otherwise occupied— a family of four having a leisurely lunch. They glanced up curiously at us from time to time, looking from me to Mr. Li and back to me again before returning to their food.

Back in China, Mr. Li said, he was a budding chef. As in the brigade system in European kitchens, the most lavish Chinese restaurants relied on highly regimented systems. He spent years training in *yue cai,* Cantonese cooking, refining his skills in some of the biggest restaurants around Beijing. These were restaurants with hundreds, sometimes thousands, of seats. (A restaurant called Xihulou in Hunan is often described as the largest restaurant in the world, with 5,000 seats and over 300 chefs). The restaurants had multiple dining rooms, spread across multiple floors and escalators in between.

Mr. Li worked in some of these huge restaurants, with their multiple kitchens, alongside hundreds of other cooks. Each cook had honed their skills for several years in each specific function. One would wash the vegetables. Another wielded the steamers. Yet another was in charge of stir-fries. Others simply ran back and forth between those cooks, fetching spoons or dishes or fresh ingredients. It all came together in a finely tuned system to ensure each and every dish came out precisely the way it had for hundreds of years.

In China, *authenticity* wasn't the question. It was just about *tradition*.

Then Mr. Li arrived in Drumheller. Suddenly he had to grapple with a new world: a new language, a new country and a new city. He knew he'd have to learn to do things all over again. But he hadn't expected cooking to be one of those things. In his cooking skills, at least, he'd been confident.

But when he arrived in his uncle's kitchen, he said, he was befuddled. He barely recognized any of the dishes on the menu. He watched, puzzled, as his uncle and the other cooks used techniques that would have gotten him fired from any kitchen in China—deep-frying seafood, or covering fresh vegetables with heavy sauces. He watched the cooks call these new dishes "lemon chicken" and "chop suey."

At first he pushed back. He tried to introduce dishes like *mapo tofu* or *laziji* to the menus. Some customers were polite and would at least try them—their grins melting into grimaces as soon as he looked away. This was a blue-collar town not known for adventurous diners. Most of his customers had lived in Drumheller all their lives and worked on farms, or at the nearby oil fields, or at the Drumheller Institution, a medium-security prison in town. (According to Statistics Canada, over half of all adults in Drumheller have no post-secondary education, with a high school diploma or less). Most of them stuck with what they knew.

Each day, he'd pack up the leftovers, boxes and boxes worth, to bring home. Gradually, he stopped trying. "Chinese food"— now he was talking about the authentic stuff—"it's very hard to make," he said. "If they don't like it, I don't want to waste too much time on it." So he, too, learned how to deep-fry seafood and slather dishes in thick sauces. It's what the people want, he figured. Might as well give the people what they want.

By this point, we'd been talking for almost half an hour. The dining room was entirely quiet now, after the last of the lunch crowd had asked for their cheques and left. In the back of the dim dining room, Mr. Li's father-in-law's head was craned toward the TV news, set to mute.

Mr. Li sighed. He'd just returned to China for a visit, he said. "In China right now," he said slowly, choosing his words carefully, "It's really good."

In the time since he and Ms. Xie left, many of their old friends had risen to China's new middle class, carried by a booming Chinese economy. Mr. Li's old friends were now in cooking positions at five-star hotels and famous Beijing restaurants. They lived fast-paced lives in China, surrounded by modern conveniences and modest luxuries. Many of them owned brand-new flats and carried around the latest smart-phones. They lived comfortable lives.

Here in Canada, meanwhile, they had arrived just as Alberta's economy began to sink. One by one, their customers were losing their jobs. Each day, the dining room was quieter and quieter. The cost of food kept rising.

Here they were in this town, Mr. Li said, switching to English: "Nothing too exciting. Every day, same same." He held his arms in the air, gesturing around the restaurant to illustrate.

Their timing had been all wrong.

As he spoke, Ms. Xie reappeared at his side. I asked her if she had friends in town, and she nodded yes, though not convincingly. "Some of the customers here are very nice," she said, quietly.

Were there other Chinese-speaking families living in the city? People she could speak with comfortably?

She counted in her head.

"I think—seven or eight?" she said.

"Seven or eight families?"

"Seven or eight people."

Her response stunned me. I couldn't imagine what that would be like. (Later, when I looked up the census figures for Drumheller, they showed that, of 6,400 or so residents in the city, only ten listed Chinese as their first language.)

"Is it lonely?" I asked.

She stayed silent for a long time.

"Of course, when we first came here, it felt very lonely," she said.

A few moments, she added, as if it were an afterthought, "Now, we feel better."

She didn't seem convinced. I knew I wasn't.

• • • • • • •

75

By the time I was getting ready to leave the Diana, Anthony had come into the restaurant to wait for me. He'd gone for a walk around the town, but found that most of the streets were empty. We walked out together toward the car, and as we drove away, I thought about what Mr. Li had said, about how confused he'd been by the "Chinese" food he'd found in Drumheller. It was the same reaction I'd had to my Chinese New Year lunch all those years earlier.

It was clear this was a made-in-North-America cuisine. But who had created it? And how much of it was Canadian?

At the Diana, one of the dishes on the menu had caught my eye. I had noticed it back at Amy's too. There, the chafing dish labelled "ginger beef" had been almost completely empty, which I took as a sign that it was a popular item. Before coming to the Prairies, I'd never before heard of ginger beef. But from what I could tell, it was a Prairie specialty.

I thought it might help me understand the origins of this "chop suey" cuisine, especially the Canadian kind. So I called up the Silver Inn Restaurant in Calgary, where ginger beef had allegedly been invented. Kwong Cheung, the restaurant's owner, picked up the phone. He chuckled when I asked about the dish. He was used to telling the story.

The Silver Inn Restaurant was first opened in Calgary in 1975 by Mr. Cheung's sisters, Lily and Louise, he told me. It was a chop suey restaurant, like almost all Chinese restaurants at the time. At the Silver Inn and at Chinese restaurants across North America—in Chinatowns in San Francisco, or New York, or Vancouver—there were only so many Chinese customers. Survival was dependent on winning over white customers. And despite an interest in "exotic" foods, many non-Chinese customers at the time still wanted flavours and ingredients that were somewhat familiar: sweet or salty or a little bit sour. They weren't ready for tongue-numbing spices or slimy textures. They were adventurous, but only a little.

Many of the first chop suey restaurant owners were used to thinking on their feet. Most of those restaurant owners weren't even trained chefs. Many had only started restaurants because they had no other options, because the work didn't require formal training or much English, and also because until the mid-twentieth century, they had been barred from other professional occupations. These cooks had learned through improvising and by copying others.

Even if they wanted to create *authentic* Chinese food, many of the ingredients they would have needed—spices, sauces or varieties of fresh produce or seafood—were difficult to find in North America anyway. So again, they improvised. Based on the ingredients available to them, they concocted new dishes they thought might appeal to Western audiences. They borrowed from the recipes and flavours they remembered back home, but added healthy doses of soy sauce and ketchup and sugar to appeal to Western tastes.

Thus was born chop suey—in other words, "bits and pieces" or "scraps." The dish was the only constant you would find in every chop suey restaurant from coast to coast. It could vary from place to place and city to city. Some used green cabbage while others had napa. Others substituted carrots or celery. Sometimes it was beef chop suey, or chicken chop suey, or vegetable chop suey. The only ingredient that was always there was bean sprouts. Bean sprouts could be grown anywhere so long as there was water. As long as you have water and a bucket, you can grow bean sprouts.

Chop suey. In other words, whatever happened to be available.

Gradually, this ad hoc cuisine became standardized. One dish would become so popular that customers would start asking for it everywhere. And then suddenly every restaurant was serving the same dish. The most popular American chop suey dishes, many of them created in San Francisco's Chinatown, spilled over the border to Canada, like chop suey itself, and General Tso's chicken.

But there were important Canadian contributions too.

Mr. Cheung explained. Ginger beef was created in the mid-1970s by his brother-in-law George Wong, he told me. It came to him while brainstorming new menu ideas.

Mr. Wong was running the restaurant with his wife, Lily (Mr. Cheung's sister), and business was decent. But like any restaurant owner, he knew he'd have to increase alcohol sales to be profitable. So he hoped that new menu items, such as smaller dishes and snack-type plates, might help.

Mr. Wong was originally from Hong Kong and had spent several years working in Peking-style restaurants. There was one Peking-style dish in particular that came to mind: a beef dish that was sweet and chewy, almost like beef jerky. It was popular back in China, often eaten as a snack. He put the dish on the menu with high hopes.

But the reactions were lukewarm. Most of the customers were white. Most were accustomed to tender Alberta beef. To them, the idea of chewy beef seemed odd. And the spices, the ginger and chilies and garlic Mr. Wong had used, were too intense for the Calgary palates.

So he went back to the kitchen.

After testing out a few different recipes, Mr. Wong had a moment of inspiration. His customers loved fried foods. "He thought, 'Why not make it a French fry?'" said Mr. Cheung.

So Mr. Wong tried it: he coated thin strips of beef in a thin batter, then deep-fried the strips to create a crisp outer layer. He was careful to avoid overcooking, so the inside of the meat stayed tender, highlighting the fresh, local beef. Then he tossed everything in a sweet chili-ginger-garlic mix, toning the spices down just a bit from the original version.

It was, like all good chop suey dishes, the perfect combination of sweet, salty, tangy and crunchy. It had some of the "exotic" Chinese flavours the customers were looking for, but blended with familiar "Western" ideas.

As soon as customers tried it, they loved it. It was an instant hit.

Thanks in large part to the popularity of the dish, the Silver Inn became massively popular. And like any good idea in a Chinese restaurant, its signature recipe was replicated.

As the dish spread across the Prairies, there was one key difference between the copycats and the Silver Inn original. At the Silver Inn, the dish was simply known as "deep-fried shredded beef with chili sauce." But though many customers tried and loved it, few could remember its name. There weren't many others cooking with chili at the time, so the customers didn't recognize the flavour. They mistook the spiciness for ginger, and began asking Chinese restaurants across the Prairies for "that beef with the ginger stuff."

Thus "ginger beef" was born.

Mr. Cheung runs the Silver Inn now, and in the decade since the dish was created, he said the restaurant cycled through about a dozen cooks. He'd recruit a qualified cook from Hong Kong, apply for the cook to come to Canada and teach him the full repertoire of Silver Inn recipes, including ginger beef. But each time, within about six or seven months, the cooks would leave.

"They'd say, 'This is popular. I can make money. Why am I cooking for you?'" said Mr. Cheung. And each time, the cook would go off and start his own Chinese restaurant featuring ginger beef.

Within years, there were Peking-style Chinese restaurants all over Calgary, all of them serving ginger beef. And soon, there was ginger beef all over the Prairies.

I told Mr. Cheung how so many of the Chinese restaurants we'd visited in the Prairies had ginger beef on the menu.

He chuckled.

"In hindsight, we should have patented that name," he said. Mr. Wong was initially "a little bit bitter" about the whole thing. But eventually, he and the entire family changed their thinking. Now they're proud of their contribution to history. "It's a uniquely Canadian dish," Mr. Cheung said.

"Never mind whether there's something kind of like it in China or Hong Kong or England. There's no other country I know of that serves ginger beef the way we serve it," he said.

"Ginger beef is uniquely Canadian."

Jingweicun, Guangdong, China.

1952-60

W ITH YE YE away in Canada, Dad was sent off to live in Guangzhou.

The schools in cities were better than the ad-hoc village ones, Dad told me. The money Ye Ye sent back from Canada gave him the luxury of continuing with his studies. So as soon as he was old enough, they sent him off. There, he lived with his grandfather, Ah Gong, and with Sook Gong, who was technically his uncle, but just two years older, and more like a brother.

Ah Gong had eventually stopped travelling abroad for work and settled in the city, where construction work was easier to find. Still, it wasn't enough to support a family, so Bak Bak and Ah Ngeen stayed behind on the farm in Jingweicun.

After a few years, Dad was used to his routine. During the school year, he was in Guangzhou. And during the summers and holidays, he and Sook Gong would return to Jingweicun. At first, Dad would look forward to these visits back to Jingweicun. In the city, he shared a hundred-square-foot bedroom with both Ah Gong and Sook Gong. The house itself they shared with another family, the Laus. All their meals were cooked in a shared kitchen and the house didn't have a washroom, so both families had to walk several minutes to get to the nearest public toilet.

But in Jingweicun, Bak Bak and Ah Ngeen had their own house. It was a mud-brick home with dirt floors and walls made of packed earth and it was dark inside no matter the time of day, but it was no better or worse than everyone else's around them. And it was all theirs—no sharing.

Outside, there was no limit to how far Dad and his friends could run. There were green rice fields as far as the eye could see, and neighbours' farms they could spend all day exploring. Dad's family's property was about one-tenth of an acre. In front of the house, facing the main dirt road, Bak Bak grew big leafy bundles of bok choy, *choy sum* and spindly stalks of sweet peas. Out toward the fields, she grew the chalky brown yams they ate with almost every meal. And a plot of land about ten minutes away was filled with waist-high peanut plants.

The trips home to Jingweicun for Chinese New Year, in the dead of winter, were less idyllic. None of the houses had heat and most people couldn't afford *meen laps*—handmade winter coats padded with cotton. So everyone would gather outside their houses each morning, sitting with their faces turned toward the sun to stay warm. "Winter suntanning," they called it.

At least at Chinese New Year there was chicken. It would be flapping its wings, terrified, when Bak Bak rounded it up, grabbing both feet in one hand. She would butcher the bird herself, plucking out its feathers and cleaning it before poaching it whole—head, feet and all—in simmering water. *Bak tseet guy,* it was called. "White cut chicken." The meat, served with ginger-scallion sauce, would be plump and juicy. And the poaching water would later be served as soup.

But the summers. Summers in Jingweicun meant sweet, juicy *longan,* a tree fruit similar to lychee, with a soft brown shell you peel off before biting into the musky white flesh. And sugar cane, which grew in tall green stalks on the neighbours' fields. Dad would spend hours with Sook Gong, gnawing on the stalks, spitting out the gristly bits and sucking greedily at the syrup.

Summers meant swimming in the lake. Together with the other kids from the village—about four of them in total—they would march off to the lake each morning. Once there, they would take turns sticking their feet in the water, moving them in circles in search of clams.

"*Wun do!*" they would scream when their foot landed on one. "*Wun do ah!*" The others would dive headfirst into the water to retrieve it. Sometimes the clams were as big as dinner plates. Other times, they were so puny they'd throw them back in. The good ones went into a bucket to bring home and make into soup. Some days they would catch several. Some days, none.

Other days, they'd spend hours at the edge of the lake, digging their hands and feet into the mud in search of catfish. Any fish bigger than a few inches long they'd take home—a prize. Dad's relationship with Ah Ngeen always felt distant, likely because of all the time he spent away. But dinner was a time they spent together, and he was proud when he had something to contribute.

But the summer when he was eleven, Dad learned Ah Ngeen, too, had left.

Normally he would arrive to find Ah Ngeen in the house waiting for him. But this time when he walked around— through the kitchen and bedroom and back outside—she was nowhere to be found.

He turned to Bak Bak.

"Where's Ah Ma?" he asked.

"Away," was all she said.

"Away for how long? Where?"

It took a while before she finally said it. "Gold Mountain," she told him. "To join your father."

He pressed her for more details, but she was vague in her response.

Something about paperwork, she said. Something about separate applications and separate residences. Something about Ye Ye's documents. None of it made much sense to him.

• • • • • • •

I studied Dad's expression as he recalled this. We were sitting on the floor of the basement, surrounded by boxes of old photos and documents. His face was blank. His eyes unmoved. He described it all so matter-of-factly.

I couldn't understand it. I thought back to my own memories of Ye Ye and Ah Ngeen. We didn't see them often growing up. Our relationships had always been distant owing to language and to Dad's stiffness around them. But I had seen that they cared. I had seen it in the dishes Ah Ngeen cooked for our visits, and in how Ye Ye always seemed to have sugar cane on hand to treat my sisters and me with. I'd seen how overjoyed Ah Ngeen had been when my aunts Jennie and Janice had their own kids—how her face lit up with delight around her new grandchildren.

I couldn't see how they could have left Dad behind by choice. But he wasn't offering any explanations.

So instead, I asked about him.

I thought back to being eleven years old, of being ferried around to piano lessons, to swimming lessons. At that age, I followed Mom around everywhere. I was completely dependent on her for everything.

"Weren't you upset when you found out she'd left?" I asked.

He was quiet for awhile.

He had no idea how far they'd gone, he said. The idea of Canada was meaningless to him. His situation was no different from his classmates whose parents worked in a neighbouring village, or the others who had smuggled away to Hong Kong.

Anyway, most of his life was in Guangzhou by then, he said. He'd already grown used to Ye Ye being gone. Now only one more person had left. Ah Gong, Sook Gong and Bak Bak were his family.

He said this all as if the matter was settled. But I wasn't convinced.

I recalled a story he'd told me just days earlier, about the one and only time he and Sook Gong had fought. It had been shortly after Ah Ngeen left, he said. That day, Ah Gong had returned home with a treat for Dad: a brand-new ruler to use at school. Small luxuries like that—school supplies or new clothes—were unheard of for them, and Sook Gong brooded jealously next to Dad.

"You only spoil him because his parents didn't want him," Sook Gong grunted at Ah Gong.

Hearing this, Dad lunged at Sook Gong. Soon both boys were tumbling on the floor, flailing around and throwing punches in every direction. I guessed the comment had struck a nerve.

So I pressed on. But Dad only grew defensive. He didn't want to discuss it any further.

"I really didn't even understand what was happening," he said. "When you're eleven, you're like a lump of rice." It was a typical deflection tactic for Dad: Try to crack a joke to distract me.

He switched to English. "No feelings." He put his two palms up to signal the conversation was over.

Stony Plain, AB.

Spring 2016

NTHONY AND I left our Edmonton hotel early to make it to our morning meeting. The meeting was set for 9:30 with the mayor of the town of Stony Plain, which was about forty minutes outside of the city.

It was a town with a population of about sixteen thousand, many of them farmers and their families. The town was first settled back in 1881 and christened "Dog Rump Creek." (It was later renamed, according to local historians, by a pioneer who wisely suggested that "Stony Plain" might be more appealing.

We pulled up outside of a brown brick building attached to a small hotel on the town's main road. "Bing Restaurant No. 1," the sign outside said. We walked inside, into a large dining room with red vinyl tables and wooden chairs. A young woman stood behind the cash register, and we told her we were there to meet with the mayor. A few minutes later, the bespectacled face of William Choy popped out from the window to the kitchen. He smiled and apologized that he was running late. He was wearing a grease-splattered apron.

Mr. Choy, forty-two, was the mayor of Stony Plain. But he was also the owner of the town's Chinese restaurant.

It was a Saturday morning and the dining room was filled with people. A group of men in flannel shirts and baseball caps sat next to cups of coffee. An elderly couple huddled over a newspaper. And at the back of the dining room, through the window, their mayor scrambled around in the kitchen, keeping an eye on the woks and checking on orders. A few minutes later, Mr. Choy, clad in a red T-shirt, the apron still tied around his waist, came out to greet us. Coffee pot in hand, he apologized that he'd be just a few more minutes. He then set about refilling cups.

When he finally sat down, I asked him about juggling his two jobs. He nodded his head, thinking. He relied a lot on his family, he said, including both of his parents and many of his extended relatives who pitched in when he had to dash out for a meeting or a community event. It was a family restaurant, not just his. But in a way, he'd spent his entire life juggling the restaurant and his outside life. This restaurant, founded by his grandfather Bing Choy in 1970 and later run by William's dad, Fon Choy, was where he had grown up.

He walked me through the kitchen, past the wide wok station with room for three woks. He gestured toward a small room off to the side, filled with boxes of restaurant supplies and equipment. As a kid, "This is where I spent most of my time," he said. William's parents spent all their time at the restaurant, and so did he.

He pointed to the desk where he had done most of his homework after school. When he was done with homework or just needed a break, he'd go out to the kitchen to visit with his dad, or help out in the dining room, refilling coffee or running orders to the tables. Even during the school day, he'd come home during lunch break to wash dishes. That was the restaurant's busiest time, and he was expected to pitch in. "That was our free time, I guess," he said. "Working." There wasn't a trace of irony in his voice.

From there, he led me down a narrow staircase, into the dim basement. It was unfinished, and mostly used as extra storage space for the kitchen. Boxes of dried egg noodles and large bags of rice were stacked against the edges. This was where he had played, he said. The rare times he had friends over, this was where they would hang out. They'd use the boxes and bags of ingredients as props in their games of hide and seek. I asked if that was strange for the other kids and their parents—for them to be playing in the basement of a restaurant. But he shook his head. Most of his friends lived on farms, he explained. When he played at their homes, they were climbing and hiding around bales of hay. It wasn't all that different.

We sat down at a table in a second dining area, a large space Bing's used to host banquets and other community events. Today, it was empty. Anthony sat down next to me. William was the first English-speaking restaurant owner we'd encountered so far, and Anthony was happy to finally be able to follow along with the conversation.

I asked William about the black-and-white framed photographs that were hung up all over the dining room. "Fengman in Guangdong," he said. "That's where we're from." His grand-father Bing had started the restaurant in 1970, but it wasn't until the restaurant was successful that he brought the rest of his family over from China. William and his parents came to Canada in the winter of 1980. William was six.

He doesn't remember much about his first days in Canada. He's pieced together bits and pieces from the images in his own mind and what relatives have told him. They say he wasn't happy about coming here, about leaving behind one set of grandparents and meeting a new set he'd never even realized existed. He doesn't remember being unhappy, though.

He does remember that some kids wouldn't play with him or his brother when they first started school. They were the only Chinese kids there, and didn't speak English. But other kids did play with them—mostly just the girls. "We were different," he said, with a shrug.

Anyways, it all sorted itself out a year or two later, he said, when the other boys realized William liked sports too.

"Then it was, 'No, you're not that different after all.'"

If anything, his parents probably had a harder time adjusting, he said. William and his brother were simply pulled aside for an hour each day in school, shown English-language flash cards and taught their ABCs. Soon, they were speaking as fluently as anyone else in town. But Jean and Fon arrived as fully-formed adults. Locals tried to pitch in, coming by the restaurant and offering them short English lessons while they ate. "Cheque," they would say, pointing to the cash register. "Cup," they said, pointing to the dishware. "Coffee." But even now, Jean spent most of her days in the kitchen, preparing food and avoiding the dining room because of her limited English.

William graduated from university with a degree in teaching in the late 1990s. But the economy was sputtering. Finding a job would have meant leaving Stony Plain, his family and his community. Instead, he stayed, continuing to work at the restaurant. In 1997, he officially took over as owner.

Since then, he's spent almost all of his days here. In the mornings, he chatted with his customers and neighbours as he poured them coffee. When they came by in large groups for lunch, he'd listen in as they complained about their days and traded gossip. Bing's was not only one of the most popular restaurants in town, but one of the only restaurants in town. "It's the heart of the town," one of the regulars told us.

Bing's was where people went to gather, to trade news and talk about what was going on in the neighbourhood. And William had the front seat for all of it.

Over time, he'd become a fixture in Stony Plain. So in 2007, he ran for and won a seat on the town council. In 2010, he was re-elected. And in 2012, he ran for mayor and won. He's held the seat since. The restaurant, it had turned out, had been the perfect launching pad for his political career.

For a few minutes, I sat back and watched as Anthony and William chatted. About half a year before our meeting, Justin Trudeau's Liberals had ousted Stephen Harper's Conservatives from the federal government. Stony Plain's local Conservative MP at the time, Rona Ambrose, had risen to become the interim federal party leader. Anthony and William chatted for a few minutes about what they thought might happen next, whether Ms. Ambrose might want to stay in the role or move on, as rumoured, to provincial or municipal politics.

At that point, I interjected, looking directly at William. "Would you ever consider running either provincially or federally?" I asked.

He didn't seem taken aback by the question. I suspected he'd been asked about it in the past.

Ever the politician, he remained coy. He didn't say yes, but he didn't say no either.

Instead, he just smiled. Smiled, I took it, because he knew that all of those opportunities were open to him.

"The door's not closed," he said.

Guangzhou, China.

1961–65

$\mathcal{T}$ HE YEAR DAD turned twelve, Ah Gong gave him a new chore. "You'll be the cook," he said.

Everyone had to have a job, Dad said. Sook Gong already had other chores, and that left cooking to Dad.

Had he shown an interest in cooking at the time? A favourite food?

Dad let out a bitter laugh. "Who had a favourite food?" he said. "We were grateful to have any food."

The house they shared with the Laus had just three bedrooms inside. The kitchen was outdoors, at the end of a shared corridor, and covered with a metal awning that hung off the building. It wasn't much, just a round charcoal stove. Everything else—buckets of water, pots and bowls—he would haul out from inside the house.

For the first few days, Ah Gong stood beside Dad, showing him how to light and tend to the charcoals. "The art of *tai foh,*" Ah Gong called it. Watching the fire. That was the trickiest, most important part. Ah Gong showed him how to use a match to burn bits of scrap wood and paper. Once he had a small flame, he would light the charcoals, using a hand-held fan to help things along. Depending on the wind and how much kindling they had, this could take anywhere from a few minutes to half an hour.

The more time Dad spent in the kitchen, the better he got at watching the fire. Eventually, he could tell just by looking at the charcoals whether the temperature was right. At a glance, he could see from the intensity of the glowing amber stones whether a pot of rice was likely to burn. The steam rising from the pot and the nutty smell of jasmine wafting through the air were all he needed to know the rice was ready.

With the rice cooked, he would heat the wok until it was searing hot. Into the wok he would pour a bit of oil, then drop in a colander's worth of freshly washed vegetables. The wok would hiss and sizzle as he poked gingerly at the greens with a pair of chopsticks, trying to avoid the oil splatter. Eventually, they'd wilt and glisten brightly. When everything was finished, he would leave a pot of water on the stove to come to a slow boil before the charcoal died down. No use in wasting a good fire.

"*Hoi toi*," Dad would shout. Prepare the table! This was the signal to Sook Gong to pull out the table, normally folded away between meals in their cramped apartment.

Each month, Ah Gong received *liangpiao*, government-issued coupons for their food allotment. For the three of them, that meant about twenty-five pounds of rice and about one pound of meat (usually pork). Vegetables didn't require coupons, so day after day, lunch and dinner were more or less the same meal: steamed rice and vegetables. Twice a day, Dad made this meal. Every day. Burning bits of wood and paper. Lighting the charcoal stones. Simmering rice on a stove. Watching the fire. Boiling the water.

He didn't know it then, but this training would prove useful over and over again.

• • • • • • •

As Dad and I sifted through the photographs in Dad's basement, one caught my eye. It was a black-and-white image, showing a girl with a ruddy face and pigtails, about sixteen, pouring a wooden bucket into a large trough to feed pigs. In the background, two young men had poles propped on their shoulders with baskets filled with rocks on either end. It looked like something out of *National Geographic*.

"Who are these people?" I asked.

"My classmates," he said.

He explained how he had reached high school just as the country began undergoing rapid change. Mao and his Red Guards were purging "imperialists" and suspected "elites" from the government. Students were forced to relocate from their schools in the cities to work the land in the villages. Dad and his classmates were mandated to spend part of the year helping out at rice farms during harvest.

Starting in high school, Dad would travel twice a year along with his entire class to a small village a few hours outside the city. This was a photo from one of those trips.

From dawn to dusk, the group would work out on the fields, harvesting rice and planting vegetables. The students would wade out into the rice paddies and spend hours hunched, cutting the stalks individually with a knife and pulling them out, one by one. At night, they would fall asleep in a giant common room on cool beds made of grass and hay, covered with bedding and blankets they brought themselves.

"Grass?" I asked.

Their beds were made of grass, strewn on the ground to soften the surface, he explained. "It was gruelling labour."

Luckily, he explained, he was spared from the worst of it.

The first year they made the trip to the rice farms, Dad happened to be a class representative, a student councillor of sorts. His teacher had taken a shine to him and also knew that Dad could cook. So each day, as his classmates set out for another hot, sweaty day in the rice paddies, Dad was assigned to stay behind and cook. Preparing three meals a day for dozens of people in a hot kitchen wasn't easy, but he was far better off than his classmates, who came back each night with dirt-streaked faces and aching muscles.

Every day, he cooked the same three meals. For breakfast, a boiled yam. For lunch, steamed vegetables with rice. For dinner, more vegetables and rice. With the money pooled together for food, Dad would make daily trips to the market for fresh vegetables and rice. And each day, he would set a bit aside, so that at the end of each week, he could afford to splurge on a few pounds of pork for everyone—a treat. These meals his classmates would eat gratefully, gulping down the accompanying soup with giant slurps.

But it wasn't enough to buy everyone's goodwill. One day, he woke up in the morning to ready the pot of water for the yams. As he set to work, he heard one of the other boys in his class loudly grumbling.

"Each day, we go out and work, and he gets to stay inside," the boy said, pointing and glaring at Dad. "It's not fair."

The teacher thought about it for a moment. It *wasn't* fair, he decided. So he had the two of them switch places. The classmate stayed behind to cook the meals and Dad set out along with the rest of his classmates to work in the fields.

Just as Dad suspected, it was back-breaking work. As he gripped the knife to cut the rice stalks one by one, his hands began to ache. His lower back soon grew sore from standing in the same position. By the time he sat down for lunch, his arms and legs felt like they were on fire. And, like everyone else, he was starving.

They marched into the lunch room, grumpy and tired, watching greedily as the bowls of steamed rice and vegetables were brought out. As soon as Dad received his bowl, he lifted it gratefully to his mouth. But from the first whiff, it was clear something wasn't right. Instead of jasmine, the rice smelled acrid. He looked closer at the bowl. Some of the rice grains were fluffy and white, but others were hard and crunchy, their centres still translucent and raw. The rice had been cooked unevenly. Others around Dad noticed too. A few cursed under their breaths.

The boy who had cooked the meal glanced around uneasily, slumping down in his seat. Everyone grumbled, but they were tired and hungry and finished their meals anyway. They still had work to do.

But hours later, another disappointment.

At dinner, the rice bowls, normally heaping full, were barely filled to the tops. The classmates murmured, confused. But Dad took in the rice bowls, and the smell that was wafting from the bowl, and figured out what had happened. The boy had burnt the rice. The meagre portions were all he had managed to salvage. Unlike Dad, this boy had not spent hours learning to *tai foh*. He did not know, as my father did, how to tell just from the colour of the charcoal whether the fire might cause the water to boil. He did not know what shade of amber would lead to burnt rice. And the pitiful portions in everyone's bowls had proved that.

After that, there were no other complaints. Dad was reassigned to the kitchen.

Boissevain, MB.

Spring 2016

W HILE PLANNING THE trip, I became obsessed with trying to find a single answer that could explain the spread of Chinese restaurants across the country. I wondered if there was a single starting point or a single place responsible for the ubiquity and uniformity of these tiny restaurants.

The Fortune Cookie Chronicles: Adventures in the World of Chinese Food by Jennifer 8. Lee traces the activities of many Chinese restaurants in the United States back to a small area of New York City's Chinatown under the Manhattan Bridge. In that Chinatown, she writes, a handful of Chinese employment agencies are clustered around a single bus station. There, restaurants and restaurant jobs are posted on bulletin boards. Entire lives and families are uprooted and rearranged over long-distance calls at a phone booth, often ending with the question: "Can you leave tonight?" Each day, Chinese men and women arrive at the agencies with their suitcases packed, prepared to jump on a bus to a new job and new city at a moment's notice.

I hoped I might find a similar phenomenon in Canada—
a single place that connected all of our Chinese restaurants. A
single place that could explain how a woman like Ms. Lin had
wound up in Vulcan, or Ms. Xie in a place like Drumheller.
Already I had lurked around the Chinese travel agencies in
Vancouver's Chinatown, looking for signs of Chinese restaurant workers buying bus tickets. Each time I saw a bulletin
board at a Chinese restaurant or store, I stopped to scan for
job listings. I scoured the Chinese newspapers, looking for
restaurant postings.

Earlier in my research, Henry Yu, a University of British
Columbia (UBC) history professor, had warned me not to
get my hopes up.

"The bus depot is ephemeral," he said. "It could be a bus
depot, or a port, or a Chinatown."

Here in Canada, he said, the spread of restaurants didn't
happen in a straight line. "It's nodal," he told me. Major cities
became main nodes for the early Chinese immigrants—cities
with convenient coastal locations, like Victoria or Vancouver.
With the railway, those Chinese communities pushed farther
east too. Often entire villages or families would wind up in
specific areas: the Chows from Hoiping settled in Vancouver;
the Tsangs settled in Toronto; the Wongs in Kenora, and so
on and so on.

And then, from each of these cities, the restaurants spread
too. One family would start a restaurant in Edmonton. Their
cousins, sometimes with the assistance of their family in
Edmonton, would move just outside of the city, to Spruce
Grove. And then to Spring Lake. Then Carvel. Then Duffield.

Across decades, the restaurants spread and spread. First it was just men from the *siyup* counties, but eventually they came from all over China. There was no limit on the number of young men and women who wanted to take a chance at working for themselves.

They spread and spread, until there was a Chinese restaurant in just about every town across Canada.

Initially it happened through word of mouth—letters sent via air mail and carefully timed long-distance calls. Now, much of it has moved online. After talking to Professor Yu, I grew curious and searched online for "Chinese restaurant for sale." The search turned up ad after ad, many of them on sites like Craigslist and Kijiji, for restaurants priced any-where between tens of thousands of dollars (for the business and not the building) to half-million-dollar businesses near major cities.

"SOLID BUILDING," read an ad for the Szechuan Garden in Windsor, ON. "GOOD AND STEADY INCOME. CLOSE TO UNIVERSITY." In Gibsons, BC, a restaurant with red vinyl booths and white plastic tables was selling for $105,000. "Plenty of local traffic," the ad said. "4.3 stars on Google Reviews." And in Prince George, BC, a "Chinese/Western restaurant" was for sale. "Could be customized to a Japanese restaurant to accommodate new business."

Often the ads emphasized a lifestyle for the entire family—good schools nearby, safe communities or grocery stores. What they were advertising were not restaurants, but new lives.

In Glendon, AB, we met Lan Huynh, a Vietnamese woman selling "Chinese pierogis" in the mostly Ukrainian town of under five hundred people. (We ordered both the fried "Chinese" dumplings and regular Ukrainian perogies, served with a side of sauerkraut.) Her Vietnamese-Chinese husband had persuaded her to come to Canada, where his mother was already running Thai Woks N'go cafe. Ms. Huynh introduced us to her son, a boy with a shaved head and round face who looked about ten.

Half an hour east, we met Jeff Deng at Panda Garden in Bonnyville. He had moved first to Edmonton. But when his uncle decided to open a restaurant in Bonnyville, he followed. As we spoke, Mr. Deng's two daughters, Vivian, ten, and Vanessa, five—two mischievous-looking girls with long hair and round faces—got ahold of my notebook, and sneakily drew doodles on the lined sheets. The two girls had a bed set up in the back of the restaurant, behind the bar, where they played and took naps while their parents worked.

Ms. Lin in Vulcan, Mr. Li in Drumheller, Ms. Huynh in Glendon, Mr. Deng in Bonnyville—they were all modern-day Gold Mountain men and women. They'd all come for the same reasons. And through their network, whether it was a brother, or a sister, an aunt or a family friend, they'd wound up in these tiny towns, running these tiny restaurants. Over 150 years after the Cariboo gold rush, the Gold Mountain system was still intact.

• • • • • • •

On the sixth day of our trip, we woke up in Brandon and set out for a small town about an hour south called Boissevain.

In addition to understanding how these restaurants spread, I was still curious about why so many of them seemed to look and feel exactly the same. Already we had seen evidence of this on our trip. The same vinyl booths. Menus printed in the same font, with the same categories, and the same dishes. The same Wing's brand plum sauce.

Many of the restaurants even had the same names. (David Chen, a blogger, would later write me to share the results of a study he'd conducted on Chinese restaurant names in the United States. He found that there are over 1,770 separate, independent restaurants in the US with the exact same name: "Panda Express." Another 511 were named "China Wok." Here in Canada I was able to find, just by googling, at least seven separate restaurants sharing the latter name in south-western Ontario alone.) These were restaurants separated by thousands of kilometres, built well before the invention of the Internet made the sharing of ideas quick and easy, yet these restaurants somehow all wound up doing things almost identically. Why?

In my early research, I had found mention of the 1,600-person town of Boissevain and of Chinese laundries built there as early as 1891. I had seen photos of Boissevain's local Chinese restaurant, with its classic chop suey menu and wood-panelled walls. It seemed like the quintessential chop suey restaurant. I thought I might find some answers there.

We drove into town along one of its main streets, past an old grain elevator. We passed the town's main attraction, an eight-and-a-half-metre-tall fibreglass turtle with a green shell and orange belly named Tommy Turtle. The turtle clutched in one of its limbs a Canadian flag, and in the other an American flag, a gesture to the town's proximity to the US. Not to be outdone, the wildlife museum right beside Tommy had a giant bear statue out front, staring straight at the turtle.

We rounded the corner, past a giant lumber yard and a trucking yard, and around the corner again toward a pink and grey building with a bright yellow sign—Choy's Restaurant. As soon as I walked into the restaurant, a young woman wearing a hoodie and sneakers greeted me. I wasn't sure what to make of her. Her hair was pulled back into a ponytail and she grasped her hands shyly in front of her. She looked about eighteen years old.

"Does your family run this restaurant?" I asked her in Cantonese.

She nodded yes.

I paused for a moment, taking in the scene around us. The dining area was split into two rooms. The back room looked just as it had in the photos, with wood panelling and tables and chairs in neat rows. Perched on a ledge at the back, three familiar-looking figurines were set up. They were the three Chinese gods, or *san xing*, which I recognized from just about every Chinese household I'd ever been in growing up. The one in the middle, with the long black beard and holding a gold nugget, represented *fu*, or fortune. The one on the right held a scroll to symbolize *lu*, or status. And the one with the long white beard, carrying a lucky peach, represented *shou*, immortality or a long life.

But the room we were standing in looked more like a family room. There was only a single dining table. And on the table were remnants of what looked like the family's breakfast: some crackers, a few slices of toast and some cut-up cucumber. There were also what looked like a toddler's drawings—a child, I realized, who was likely hers.

"Are you the owner?"

She nodded again, this time a little shyly, and introduced herself as Su Fen Li.

It turned out Ms. Li was actually thirty-two years old, more or less my age. She had a four-year-old daughter, and the family treated the restaurant as an extension of their living room. She nodded to the front counter, where a gold *maneki-neko,* or "lucky cat," sat beside a flat-screen television. That was where she spent most of her time.

Ms. Li seated the two of us at a table in the dining room in the back. As we talked, I noticed her peering back and forth between Anthony and me several times, curious, as if trying to make sense of the two of us. I wondered what she thought of this person in front of her, Chinese but barely able to speak it, and her white husband. I thought how strange I must have seemed to her.

We ordered a few dishes—a Cantonese chow mein and, at her suggestion, a plate of sesame chicken. She disappeared into the kitchen to deliver the order to her husband. Then she came back out to chat with us while we waited for the food.

They had been in Canada about ten years, she said. She spoke in Cantonese, but with a heavy Toisan accent. I did the math. That would have meant she was just about twenty when she came here. She nodded. She had been running a small clothing stall in Guangzhou. Her husband was fixing air conditioners. But their relatives convinced them to come to Canada. Her husband's sister was already living in Canada, in Brandon. Her uncle, too, lived in Canada.

They worked a variety of jobs when they first arrived in Brandon, in restaurants and at the local Maple Leaf Foods pork processing plant. They also tried Toronto, where she worked for a commercial laundry company. But after an entire year there, she received only a twenty-five-cent raise—bringing up her hourly wage to $8.75. Plus the cost of living was high and the traffic was terrible. So they moved back to Brandon.

There, they settled into a string of restaurant jobs. She continued waitressing and he cooked, first at a food-court Chinese restaurant at the mall, and later at a restaurant called the Golden Dragon, where she waited tables. It was her boss at the Golden Dragon who first told her about the restaurant in Boissevain. The couple who had run it for over twenty years were retiring and looking for a new couple to take over. Were they interested?

They took a trip out to Boissevain to see the restaurant. They rounded the corner at the grain mill, drove past Tommy Turtle and turned to find the short grey building with the bright yellow sign.

She pulled her hands into the sleeves of her hoodie and shrugged. "We decided to try," she said.

When I asked her about what was on my mind—about why so many of these restaurants were so similar—she laughed. It was something she had thought about before.

Choy's was just like all of the other Chinese restaurants, she said. When they bought Choy's, they were buying the entire business, including the furniture, the equipment and all of its recipes. What the Choy family was selling them was not just a restaurant, but all of their expertise in running the restaurant. For the first month, Mr. Choy stayed with Ms. Li and her husband at the restaurant to show them how to run the business exactly the way he'd done in the past.

He spent entire days in the kitchen with Ms. Li's husband, showing him the right way to wrap a spring roll, or the right amount of batter for sesame chicken. He also handed them a dust-covered binder filled with all of the recipes they would need to cook every single item on the menu. This binder and these recipes had been passed down from the previous owner, and the previous owner before that.

At the front counter, he showed Ms. Li how to run the front of house the same way it had always been done. He showed her how to fill out a cheque to properly bill a customer. How to punch in an order on the cash register. How to order new take out menus from a supplier. Changing anything, including the name, would cost money. And the Choys had already proven their way of doing things could be successful, she said. The more he showed them, the more it became clear that it would easiest and cheapest to keep things exactly the same. And if they were ever to open a Chinese restaurant elsewhere, they'd likely do things exactly the same there too.

Now, it had been almost a year. She wasn't sure whether they would stay long-term in Boissevain. I asked if she'd had a chance to see the nearby provincial parks or lakes, or gone to the US, with the border nearby. But she just shook her head and sighed.

"We're always working," she said. "There's no time to stop."

The number of hours they spent at the restaurant didn't seem to be adding up with the amount of money they were taking home. Each morning they opened the restaurant at nine and stayed until past closing twelve hours later. Her parents looked after their daughter.

Ms. Li figured she and her husband were taking home maybe two thousand dollars each month.

"For this kind of money we may as well work for someone else."

Another idea was to head out to a bigger city, like Edmonton. They'd heard stories of restaurant owners taking home profits that seemed unimaginable—four or even five thousand dollars each month. But again she shook her head, as if to say she could never be so lucky.

"Life is made up of many decades," she said eventually. "We'll do this for now."

Guangzhou, China.

1966-74

B Y THE TIME Dad was fifteen, schools had shut down entirely.

The revolution had reached the streets of Guangzhou. He watched as the Red Guards—some of them former classmates of his, no older than he was—descended on their teachers and other "intellectuals." There were street fights. Riots. Signs of violence everywhere.

The scenes were horrifying, but he kept quiet. His own parents were abroad and thus, defectors. That made him a target too.

"Were you afraid?"

"We couldn't show our feelings," Dad said.

"But did you ever try to stop things?"

"We didn't know who was right," he said. "Nobody knew."

So he kept his head down. Most days, he and his best friend, Dsee Dai, holed up in Dsee Dai's apartment, avoiding the chaos and trying to stay out of the fray.

As he walked toward Dsee Dai's house one morning, he heard people speaking in hushed tones. They said something about a disturbance on Wende Road, where he was headed. He considered turning around and going home, but he was almost there. He paused for a few moments, listening for signs of trouble—the familiar sounds of people shouting or gunfire. But he heard nothing. So he kept walking.

As he turned the corner onto Wende Road, he saw what everyone had been whispering about.

About one hundred metres ahead of him, dead bodies, hanging limply like rag dolls from a tree. About a dozen of them.

He froze, unable to breathe or even look away.

Then he turned around and ran all the way home.

After that day, Dad and Sook Gong were sent back to Jingweicun.

Up until then, he'd held out hope he might one day become a teacher. It was a lofty goal for a kid from Jingweicun. But until then, it had still seemed possible. Ye Ye's money from Gold Mountain, the money that had allowed him to continue with schooling, had made it so.

Dad was a diligent student, naturally clever and hard-working. He was quiet and well-liked by his teachers. He looked up to them too—these men and women with their smart clothes and thick books. In his free time, he read poetry. His favourite was the famous poet Li Bai. On scrolls, he would practise calligraphy with these poems, one character after another, perfecting his strokes. He imagined one day he could be like his teachers—far, far away from the gruelling work in the fields.

But with the start of the revolution, that dream went out the window. There were no more classes, no more school. His hard work studying for exams, his careful efforts to get good grades—none of that mattered anymore. Even if the schools eventually reopened, even if things went back to normal, too much time had passed. He'd missed too much.

Now he was back in Jingweicun, back on the farms where he had begun. What small privilege he once had no longer mattered. The luxury he'd once had, the ability to dream of something better, had slipped away.

He felt insignificant. Vulnerable.

"We were all like weeds twisting in the wind," he said.

• • • • • • •

In the basement of his house in Burnaby, Dad sat on the floor surrounded by legal boxes stuffed full of papers. He was sorting through the boxes in hopes that some of the old documents and photos might be helpful to me. As he sorted, he talked.

A few years after the incident on Wende Road, things eventually calmed down in Guangzhou, he said. The schools reopened and Dad was able to move back to the city. But it was already too late. He had seen how quickly everything could be taken away. His life in China now felt fragile, and meaningless.

He picked up a photo from the floor. He studied it for a few minutes, then handed it to me. It looked familiar, but I couldn't remember where I'd seen it before.

This was a photo that arrived a few years after Ah Ngeen had left, he said. It came in the mail when he was about thirteen. It was the first he'd heard from her.

I looked at the image. It showed Ah Ngeen posing stiffly in front of a curtain, wearing a form-fitting dress and high heels. Standing next to her was Ye Ye, stern-looking in a button-up shirt and dark slacks.

"This is the first time I ever saw my dad," he said.

Those words struck me. "The first time I ever saw my dad." Ye Ye had left when Dad was just one year old. So until that photo arrived, he'd only been able to imagine what his father looked like. I imagined Dad, as a young man, studying the photograph, taking in the image of the man standing stiffly next to his mother. The man dressed in dark slacks and a white shirt. Trying to read Ye Ye's blank expression.

"What did you think?" I asked.

"I was surprised at how different Ah Ngeen looked," he said.

I could see what he meant. Instead of her drab village clothes, she was wearing a dress that had been neatly pressed. Her hair had been permed and carefully styled. There was something about the image that haunted me. The way they were stiffly posed, the clothes they were wearing, their blank gazes. It didn't look like a photo that had been taken just to show to Dad, and family and friends. It looked like it had been taken in an office somewhere. I imagined a professional photographer, in a suit and tie, instructing them on how to pose. It looked like something official. But why?

The photo haunted Dad too, but for a different reason. Seeing Ah Ngeen with her permed hair and fancy clothes, it suddenly dawned on him that where she'd gone to, Canada, must be a very different place. That her life—both her and Ye Ye's lives—had changed dramatically.

In the time since she'd left, someone at school had shown him a map. He had finally seen just how far this place called Canada was. He finally understood that it was an entirely different country, separated by an ocean and many countries in between.

He wondered what his parents' lives were like in that new country. Whether they ever felt as hopeless as he did. In their letters, they'd written that they'd given birth to two babies in Canada. They taped a Chinese yuan to one of the letters. "This is from your sisters," it said.

They'd built new lives and a new family in this new place. He wondered if they ever thought about him, a weed twisting in the wind.

· · · · · · ·

Just like it had for Ye Ye, Dad's invitation to Gold Mountain came in the form of a letter.

Around 1972, when he was about twenty-one, he received a letter from Ye Ye.

He was urging Dad to fill out paperwork to start the process to immigrate to Canada. Whatever complication had formerly stood in the way of bringing Dad to Canada had eased. Dad was skeptical. He was ready to leave, but cautious about getting too excited and having his dreams dashed.

But Ye Ye seemed hopeful. "Just fill out the application and see what happens," he wrote.

What Dad didn't know was that Canada had elected a new prime minister, a young man named Pierre Trudeau who had established a policy of "multiculturalism" in Canada. Dad had no way of conceiving how a group of strangers in Ottawa, on the other side of the world, could suddenly change his life with a vote.

So Dad walked to the small immigration office on Sai Woo Road in downtown Guangzhou and filled out an application form. It wasn't far from the alcohol and tobacco shop where he was working full time, as a sales clerk.

And then he waited. A few months passed, and then a letter from the Chinese government telling him to return to the immigration office to fill out some more paperwork. They were giving him a passport. That wasn't in itself an approval, but it was a promising sign. So he returned to the immigration office to pick up the passport. It was a tiny, one-door office without even a sign on the door. After that, he kept waiting. Months passed. A year. Then two.

Many nights he'd wonder about it, then push the idea out of his mind. "Don't let yourself get excited," he told himself.

All this time, he told no one, not even his closest friends or colleagues. Not even Dsee Dai. The revolution had left a lasting mark. Even close friends and neighbours could betray one another. He had seen it for himself with his classmates. He didn't want to attract any attention.

In 1974, when Dad was twenty-two, he received another letter. This one was a request for official documentation that Ye Ye was, in fact, his father. Ye Ye submitted a letter dated March 23, 1974, signed and submitted with an official Guangzhou seal: "The applicant: Hui Yam Hung, male, born April 19, 1951, living at 12 Datong Road, Guangzhou," it said in Chinese characters. "Applicant Hui Yam Hung is the son of Hui Man Yen. Hui Man Yen is the father of Hui Yam Hung."

A few months after that, he was sent for a medical exam at the local government-run clinic. At this point, he let himself get excited. He had heard from others that the results of a medical exam were only good for six months. That meant his approval was likely imminent.

Still, he kept the news to himself.

Finally, in July, an invitation from the Chinese embassy to a meeting. The morning of the meeting, he walked into a room at the embassy. Inside were about eight others sitting around a table. All of them were older than him. Some looked to be in their sixties. All of them, he learned, had also made applications to go to Canada. They all looked as nervous as he felt.

An official told him to sit, so he sat. Another brought out tea to serve to the group. They sat like that for a few minutes, nervously making small talk, until the government official cleared his throat and finally spoke.

"Once you are in Canada, you must be careful to mind your behaviour," the man said. "Do not do anything to harm the reputation of China in Canada."

At that, they all turned to each other. That was the confirmation they'd been waiting to hear. It was official. They were going to Canada.

The official directed them to talk among themselves. "Introduce yourselves to each other," he said. "Maybe you'll be able to help one another once you're there."

The woman beside Dad turned to him to introduce herself. But Dad couldn't keep up with the conversation. His mind was racing. He tried to mind his behaviour. After all, the officials were still right there, watching. He couldn't act too pleased. But still, he couldn't stop a small smile from spreading across his face.

He was going to Canada. Finally.

• • • • • • •

The night before Dad left, he went back to Jingweicun for one last visit.

He had already wrapped things up in Guangzhou. He gave Sook Gong his bicycle, what meagre savings were in his bank account and a golden phoenix ring Ah Ngeen had sent him.

Hearing that he would be leaving, neighbours and friends prepared one last dinner, heaping plates of steamed vegetables, a chicken and fish, to send him off on his journey. They took down the dividers between the rooms in Bak Bak's house and sat all twenty of them around one table, sharing stories and giving him their last pieces of advice.

"Eat more when you're there," his aunties told him. The village had just been through another famine, one of the worst ones in years. If there was food there, he should eat it, they said.

They told him to write letters to let them know how he was getting along. A few others told him, "If you have the opportunity, you should come back someday."

What none of them said to him was, *See you soon.* It didn't even seem a possibility. A few former classmates had stolen away to Hong Kong and they had never been heard from again. Forget about a place as far as Canada.

Afterward, they all sat out on the street. The classmates were mostly quiet, not knowing what to say. They had all heard stories of Hong Kong, tales of cash and gold literally lining the streets. But Canada was a complete mystery to them. Even Ah Gong, normally loud and boisterous, was quiet that night.

"Listen to your parents" was all he said. "Work hard."

The next morning, Dad woke up early to set off for the train station. His boss at the Guangzhou shop had arranged for a car to take him—a luxury. Ah Gong, Bak Bak and an aunt all rode with him. A few of his former classmates also met them at the platform.

At the station, they said their final goodbyes. Ah Gong stuttered, wiping his nose. Bak Bak began to cry. He looked at his grandparents, who had cared for him when there had been no one else. They were already getting older. The hairs around their temples were grey. *I may never see them again,* he thought.

The train arrived and he stepped on. He settled in his seat before taking one last look at his grandparents still standing on the platform. They both looked frail and small.

The train lurched into a crawl and within moments was hurtling down the tracks. Before he realized it, they were speeding ahead.

Thunder Bay, ON.

Spring 2016

O N THE EIGHTH day of our trip, we woke up in Thunder Bay, ON. I hadn't planned any restaurant visits that day, thinking the city, with a population of over 90,000, was too big to fit the definition of "small town." We had stopped there only as a way to break up the long drive between Manitoba and central Ontario.

But when we woke up that morning, the skies were grey and drizzling. Anthony was grumpy. He'd gotten two speeding tickets the day before.

We'd driven through BC and right through the Prairies without any problems. Not once were we stopped driving through the Rockies, where the speed limit reached 120 kilometres per hour and the roads wrapped around alarming hairpin turns, where we went for hours on open highway between seeing police cars.

But the moment we crossed the provincial boundary into Ontario, the limit on the highway suddenly dropped down to ninety kilometres per hour. It was a limit Anthony had a hard time sticking to. The police, who seemed to be everywhere, took notice. Within the course of a few hours, we were stopped twice. "Don't they have anything better to do than to troll the highways giving out tickets?" Anthony grumbled under his breath.

He needed cheering up, so we decided to go for pancakes.

We pulled up to Hoito Restaurant, and I double-checked that we had the right address. The restaurant was in the basement of a three-storey building otherwise labelled "Finlandia Club"—a Finnish labour temple built in the early twentieth century for the Finnish workers who settled in Thunder Bay to work in the logging camps. The club was a place for the workers to gather, and Hoito, a restaurant to give them a taste of back home.

We pulled open the doors to find a large cafeteria-style room with wooden furniture. When the pancakes arrived, Anthony's eyes grew wide.

"Whoa," he said. "I was not expecting that."

These were like no pancakes I'd ever seen. Each one was just a few millimetres thick and covered almost the entire surface area of the plate. I doused mine in syrup, then took a bite. The centres were soft and chewy, and the edges crispy. They were delicious. Despite my best efforts, I was only able to finish about a quarter of the plate.

While we sat there trying to digest our pancakes, Anthony suggested we look for a Chinese restaurant in Thunder Bay.

"Why not?" he said. "Since we're here."

I did a quick search on my phone, scanning through the results quickly. The names were all starting to blur together.

Chinese Express, Golden Wok, Oriental Garden. Beneath each name was a rating—whether customers deemed the place a two- or three-star restaurant. And beneath that was its category type. Most were simply listed as "Chinese" or "Restaurant."

But one result caught my eye.

Under category it said "Chinese, Skating Rinks."

Skating rink?

I clicked on it. Ling Lee's Chinese Cuisine, the place was called. "This place," I said, handing the phone to Anthony. "Let's go here."

Five minutes later, we pulled up to a grey building with a sign that read "Port Arthur Curling Club." Inside, we climbed up a flight of stairs to find a large, open area overlooking the ice rinks below. On one side was a wood-panelled bar, decorated with trophies and a league schedule. And on the other side was a takeout-style window with a sign: "Ling Lee's Chinese Cuisine." Next to it was a buffet table with heat lamps hung above large chafing dishes. It was a Chinese restaurant.

• • • • • • •

It was the early 1970s and the board of directors of the Port Arthur Curling Club had a problem on their hands.

Business at the rink was going well. Despite competition from another club just a ten-minute drive away, Port Arthur had its own established group of regulars, thanks to its over-eighty-year history. But it was the dining room and restaurant business on the second floor that troubled the board. They had tried running the restaurant themselves. But it wasn't making money. Over time, it had become more trouble than it was worth.

One day, some of the board members stopped in at the bar at the Dragon Room, then a popular Chinese restaurant. As usual, the place was packed. Customers flocked to the dining room for the dry spareribs ("served with spice salt and lemon wedges, $1.90") and *char suee bok toy* ("an authentic favorite").

Chinese food, by then, had become one of the most popular types of cuisine for eating out not only in Thunder Bay, but across North America. For many of the city's mostly blue-collar residents, going to a "Western" restaurant didn't make sense. They could make meatloaf or turkey sandwiches themselves at home. But Chinese restaurants were exotic. They fit with the new, more cosmopolitan worldview Canadians were beginning to develop, influenced by Nixon's visit to China, where he famously sampled from a platter of Peking duck, and the opening of Canada's doors to immigration from China, Europe and other parts of the world.

Seeing the success of the Dragon Room gave the board members an idea. They approached its manager, a young man named Ling Lee, with a proposition: Would he consider taking over the restaurant at the curling club? He agreed almost immediately.

Mr. Lee was hardly a stranger to bold decisions, his daughter, Norina Karschti, told me. She was working in the kitchen of Ling Lee's when we walked into the restaurant.

At fifteen, her father had followed *his* father from Guangdong to Saskatoon, despite not knowing any English. He slowly learned the language and, a few years later, moved to Ontario on a lark. He'd been shown a photograph of a pretty young Chinese woman and was told she lived in Kenora, ON. So he set out looking for her. By the time he turned nineteen, he and the woman in the picture, May Lee, were married.

The couple settled in Thunder Bay, where he found work in various Chinese restaurants. By his early thirties, he was managing the Dragon Room. And by the time the Port Arthur club board approached him, he was ready for a place of his own.

So he said yes. In 1973, Ling Lee's in Port Arthur Curling Club was opened.

Now Ms. Karschti ran the restaurant. After she'd finished explaining the restaurant's history, I asked her a question I hadn't yet dared ask any of the other restaurant owners. Like me, Ms. Karschti was Chinese but born in Canada. Like me, she was married to a non-Chinese husband, and spent the majority of her time around non-Chinese Canadians. She understood what it was like to navigate between the cultures.

"Is it strange to you, selling Chinese food that you know isn't *actually* Chinese?"

She chuckled.

At Ling Lee's, the specialty was "Bon Bon ribs"—a made-in-Thunder-Bay invention of spareribs coated in allspice and MSG, then deep-fried quickly and spritzed with lemon. It was one of the dishes that helped make Mr. Lee so popular he was hired by the local cable TV station to host his own cooking show. Each week, he invited viewers into his kitchen to show them the secrets of cooking "Chinese food."

She told me how her father became the face of chop suey

cuisine for Thunder Bay. He was so successful at spreading the brand that, in most Canadian minds, those chop suey dishes *were* Chinese. So eventually, when he decided he wanted to introduce Thunder Bay to another, *authentic* Chinese restaurant, the response was lacklustre.

"We tried," Ms. Karschti said. "People just didn't want to go for that."

What was originally an authentic-only menu became two, with one devoted to chop suey. And gradually, two menus became one again—chop suey dishes only.

"He was so frustrated by that."

• • • • • • •

It was nearing lunchtime, and we could hear the clanging of wok paddles banging against hot steel in the Ling Lee kitchen. The two cooks inside were busy getting the buffet ready for the lunch rush. A few regulars were already sitting at tables, watching for the lights above the buffet line to light up.

Downstairs at the curling rinks, the lights came on with a sudden click. Two men in fleece vests and pants walked out onto the ice, lining up their rocks for a game.

Ms. Karschti sat at one of the dining tables, surveying the scene. She flagged down a waitress to remind her about an upcoming visit from health inspectors.

This restaurant, and this restaurant life—it had never been part of her plan, Ms. Karschti explained to me. It was her father's dream, not hers. She had never intended to take over the family business.

But that was just it. It was a family business. Even more so than the food, she said, Chinese restaurants are defined by the families that run them.

It was something we would hear echoed over and over. The first Chinese men who opened these restaurants did so in order to create jobs for themselves. Eventually they realized the restaurants created jobs for their families too. Suddenly, they were giving themselves jobs, and also their brothers and nephews and children.

Growing up in Thunder Bay, Ms. Karschti said, her parents left her and her sister at home alone while they were working. They regularly worked sixteen-hour workdays, from about ten a.m. until about two a.m. every single day. It was her sister, eight years older, who took care of her. The year Ms. Karschti turned fourteen, her sister got married and moved away. And then she was alone.

Because of this, she wanted to get as far away as possible from the restaurant life. The restaurant was the reason why she never saw her parents. It was the reason they were always so exhausted. It was the reason why they were stuck living in this place, one of just a few Chinese families in town. And the latter was the reason why she was bullied at school and called a "chink."

She finished school and got a job with the provincial government. But in the late 1990s, around the time Ms. Karschti was in her early thirties, the ministry she worked for underwent major restructuring. It looked like she was going to lose her job. At the same time, her parents were getting older. Her dad had spent a lifetime building up the restaurant. He couldn't bear the thought of turning it over to a stranger, or worse, shutting it down. It was his legacy.

So she agreed to come help out, on a temporary basis.

But, she soon learned, the words "temporary" and "part-time" didn't seem to exist in Chinese restaurants. Nor did the idea of an eight-hour workday, or any kind of work-life balance. It was a family business, and as such, all-consuming. She was expected to be there all day, every day. From early until late.

Not long after Ms. Karschti came on board at Ling Lee's, her mother retired. And soon after, she was taking over many of her father's duties too. Soon, it was Ms. Karschti working day-to-night and spending all of her time at the restaurant. Soon, it was her kids she was leaving at home. Now, she's fifty and looking down the road at her own eventual retirement. She wonders whether she made the right decision in taking over the restaurant.

"I have huge regrets. My son is going to be nineteen, and I've barely spent time with him," she said.

Her son helps out once in a while. He talks about perhaps taking over the business someday. But unlike her own dad, Ms. Karschti isn't sure that's what she wants for her child.

It was the same thing I'd heard from other restaurant owners. That they never, ever wanted their own children to end up working in restaurants.

"Do I want to put my child through what I went through?" said Ms. Karschti.

But then she thinks about the stability the restaurant has given her family. It's hard work, but the restaurant provides a steady income and comfortable life. She figures that's the real reason her dad wanted her to take over. It was his way of making sure she was taken care of.

"My kids want for nothing. They can go to the best schools," she said. "So there's give and take, right?"

Hong Kong–
Vancouver, BC.
1974

*W*E WERE JUST starting to make dinner at my parents' house one evening when I found myself bickering with Mom over dishcloths.

Dishcloths.

The ones they had hanging from their stove were dingy and fraying at the edges. They'd been using the same two for years: one of those orange, super-absorbent dishcloths that had long since faded, and a threadbare, discoloured white one with blue border and the words "Good morning" printed in red. Seeing this, I had bought them a tube of disposable antibacterial wipes. But for months, the tube had gone unopened.

"How can you keep using these?" I said, pointing to the dirty cloths. "They're dirty and they're spreading germs. But these," I said, picking up the tube of wipes. "You haven't even touched."

Mom shrugged. "Why waste them?"

This was a common refrain for both of them. It was their response to why they never bought new clothes. It was why Dad was wearing the same paint-splattered sweaters from the 1980s, and socks so worn out they may as well have been hosiery. It was why I would often see Mom sitting hunched over the kitchen table, cutting stacks of paper napkins in half.

I found this maddening.

"Our mouths are only so big," she would say. "You don't need the whole thing."

I could never understand their thinking. They had been poor in China and in Hong Kong. And they had struggled for many years here in Canada too. But by now, they had more than they needed. They were comfortably retired, with their house paid off. Plus, they owned several investment properties on top of that. They travelled frequently and could buy just about anything they wanted. "You have the money," I said to her, exasperated. "You can buy as many dish towels as you want. New ones! Clean ones! Or tubes and tubes of these wipes!"

But they were similarly astounded by me. They'd visit our house in Toronto, shaking their heads at the leftovers we would allow to go bad in the refrigerator, or the snacks we would buy on the road instead of bringing our own. The pained expression Mom gave me when I confessed we were spending hundreds of dollars each month on a dog walker. "What a waste," she had mumbled under her breath.

There's a saying in Chinese, a *chengyu* or four-character idiom, that Mom would repeat often. Translated literally, it means: "Bitter first, sweet later." To many Chinese, and especially to

Mom and Dad, this was the natural order of things. To them, success could only come after sacrifice—and their scrimping and saving was part of that sacrifice. I thought they should begin enjoying their success, but they were still hung up on the sacrifice.

Eventually, Dad pulled me aside. "Come," he said. "Look what I found."

I followed him, watching as he scrounged around his room for a few moments, digging through the plastic bags he seemed to keep all his belongings in. Eventually, he found what he was looking for: a wool blanket, mustard yellow with a floral pattern, wrapped in a clear plastic case.

"What is this?" I asked.

"I bought this in Hong Kong," he said.

Hong Kong? I scanned my memory. He and Mom had made many trips back to China over the years. Since retiring, they'd made the trip once every couple of years. But after Dad got sick, they had slowed down with their travels. I couldn't think of a recent trip.

"Not recently," Dad said. "Back when I came to Canada."

I did the math quickly. Forty-two years. He had held onto this blanket for forty-two years?

He cleared a space beside him on the carpet, pushing a few plastic bags off to the side. Then he eased himself onto the ground and began talking.

• • • • • • •

It was about noon by the time Dad's train pulled into the station in Hong Kong. It was his first time outside of China, and from what he'd heard of the city, he expected the streets to be paved with gold.

Instead, he stepped out onto a crowded sidewalk, a mess of people all breathing in the same thick smog. The air smelled of rotting fruit and sewage. Everywhere he turned, there were crowds. As he made his way down the street, cars and taxis and buses sped by, blowing hot diesel toward him. He felt dizzy.

Clutching his suitcase beside him, he rode a bus to Central Hong Kong. There, his uncle came to meet him, taking him to a Hong Kong–style diner—a *cha chaan teng*—for lunch. Looking at the menu, Dad had no idea what to order. He didn't recognize anything on the menu. Back in the area around Jingweicun, there had been only two restaurants, one that sold congee in the morning and another that served dim sum in the afternoon.

But this diner had baked toast with sweet condensed milk, instant noodles with ham, sandwiches, cocktail buns and pork cutlets in tomato sauce. It was traditional Hong Kong–style cafe food influenced by the city's long history of British occupation. *Cha chaan tengs* exploded in popularity in the mid-twentieth century as the city's economy became more and more reliant on manufacturing and factory workers looking for a quick, cheap food during their short lunch breaks.

Dad's uncle ordered a plate of *gon chow ngau ho*, stir-fried rice noodles with beef, onion and bean sprouts. When the plate arrived, piping hot, Dad took a bite and his eyes widened. The noodles were hot, salty, greasy. They were delicious. His uncle told him he wasn't hungry, so Dad happily shovelled bite after bite into his mouth with his chopsticks. Back at Uncle's apartment inside a public housing complex in Chai Wan, he took in the cramped living area—a bed and dining table pushed so closely together they were almost touching. It wasn't that much different from Ah Gong's in Guangzhou. That was when Dad realized Uncle likely had been hungry back at the *cha chaan teng*, he just couldn't afford to order a second plate.

Dad had about a week to spend in Hong Kong, so each day he went out to explore the city, taking in the Tiger Balm Garden in Wan Chai and spending a day shopping with his aunt to buy supplies he would need in Canada. Ye Ye had sent him some money—the equivalent of about six hundred dollars Canadian. It was more cash than he'd ever seen before.

Ye Ye had warned him about the cold in Canada, so he used the money to buy a couple of sweaters, a thick jacket for the winter and a leather coat. He also bought his very first camera—a Japanese brand called Yashica, which Dad pronounced "Yes-ka."

He also bought a thick blanket, padded with cotton, with yellow and brown flowers—the blanket he was holding now. He held it up to me now, proudly. "See?" he said. He had kept it after all these years. I reached out beneath the pouch to graze the surface of the blanket. It was wool and rough to the touch. I had never seen it used in our house by Dad or anyone else.

"Why did you keep it?" I asked. He shrugged, just as Mom had earlier. "Why waste it?" he responded. Seeing Mom and I bicker earlier must have reminded him of that time. Of being young and spending six hundred dollars on clothes and cameras. He likely hadn't thought about how long it must have taken Ye Ye to save up that kind of money. He saw in me now how he'd been all those years ago.

I asked him what else he bought. He dug around his room some more, pulling open drawers and the little cloth pouches inside them. Finally, he found what he was looking for: a stainless steel wristwatch. He handed it to me. It was a Rado brand watch with a round face the size of a golf ball. "Golden Sabre," it said on the bottom.

"Ye Ye asked me to buy two watches," he said. So he'd spent one afternoon with his aunt, walking from store to store. He had no idea where to start. Would Ye Ye prefer something conservative, or flashy? He had no idea. He'd never met the man.

He wound up settling on this stainless steel design. He put one on his wrist. It was the first wristwatch he had ever worn. He liked how it felt cold and heavy on his wrist. Substantial. He decided he wanted one too, so he asked the clerk for another one—two for his dad and one for himself. He'd never made such a large purchase before. He left feeling important.

While in Hong Kong, he marvelled at how colourful the people all looked. Back in China, brightly coloured clothing, or anything that attracted attention, was frowned upon. Most people wore the same drab, work-issued black or grey garb. Besides, few households could afford the luxury of soap. Wearing dark colours was just practical. Here, people wore blue and yellow and pink and red, and clothes in all shapes and styles. They wore whatever they wanted.

• • • • • • •

On September 29, 1974, eight days after he had first arrived in Hong Kong, Dad boarded a Canadian Pacific Air Lines flight to Vancouver.

After the engines began whirring and the plane hurtled down the runway, he breathed in sharply, amazed at how effortlessly they lifted into the air. After takeoff, the flight attendant made an announcement on the PA system, but she spoke only in English. He looked around, wondering if he should ask one of the Chinese-looking faces around him. But he was embarrassed and didn't want to draw attention to himself, so he stayed silent.

For the entirety of the flight, he would stay like that, sitting silently in his seat. He had no idea when he was supposed to stand up or stay seated. He didn't know how to use the bathroom, or even that there was one. When the lights in the airplane cabin dimmed so that passengers could nap, he didn't know if he should be alarmed. Nor did he know what to make of the chiming noise that would come on over the intercom every once in a while. No one else seemed bothered by it. Each time the plane lurched, or dropped, or shook from turbulence, he let out a quiet breath, hoping that what he was hearing was normal.

At one point, a flight attendant came up to him. She looked directly at him and spoke in quick English. He stared back dumbly, feeling his face grow warm. The flight attendant repeated herself a few times, but Dad just sat frozen in his seat. Eventually, the young Chinese woman next to him pointed her finger toward a metal cart the flight attendant had parked a few rows away—a cart covered with beverage cans and metal teapots. "She's asking what you want to drink," the woman said to Dad.

He didn't want to draw further attention to himself, so he said he'd have whatever she was having. The flight attendant gave them both orange juice.

Many hours later, as they prepared to land in Vancouver, Dad stared out the window, fascinated. The ocean glittered blue below and seemed to go on forever. The houses, tiny boxes of white and grey, had neat square tracts beside them. He guessed the green fields surrounding them were farms. There was so much space.

The plane landed with a series of thuds, and afterward Dad followed everyone off the plane. He followed as they walked past signs printed in all English. He followed as they made their way down wide concourses and into a smaller lounge with line-ups and stern-looking officers sitting behind a pane of glass. When it was his turn at the glass, a translator standing over the shoulder of the officer spoke to Dad in Cantonese. "How much money are you bringing into the country?" he asked.

"Twenty-nine dollars."

"What's in your luggage?"

He listed off his belongings: Five pairs of pants. A few shirts. A leather jacket. The blanket. A camera. The watches. A moon cake.

"A moon cake?"

"It's almost mid-autumn festival," Dad explained. It was a gift for his family.

The customs official nodded as the translator explained this to him. He threw the cake out anyway.

Then he asked about the watches.

"I just bought them in Hong Kong," Dad said. He didn't understand the purpose of the interview, or why he was being asked about his belongings. When asked, he told the officer how much he'd paid for the watches. A few moments later, the two men consulted with one another, and the translator told him to wait to the side. Dad stood there, nervously. Had he done something wrong?

From behind a pane of glass, he watched the official return a few minutes later. He was accompanied by another man, Chinese, in his forties. The man wore a dark T-shirt and slacks. It was Ye Ye.

At last, here was his father. Dad watched as Ye Ye glanced at him. Their eyes met for the first time. The expression on Ye Ye's face was difficult to read. His brow was pinched together, and his lips pursed. He responded to the customs official in short bursts and huffs. He looked—*irritated*.

The two men continued to talk for a few more minutes before Dad watched Ye Ye pull a stack of bills out of his wallet. He peeled a few off and handed them to the officer. Then he turned around and left. The officials returned. "You're fine to go," the translator said.

Dad walked out the door into the arrivals lounge. They were all standing there: Ye Ye, Ah Ngeen and Great-Aunt.

Great-Aunt spoke first: "This is your dad," she said to him. "Call him 'Father.'"

Up close, Dad could see how much the man looked like him—just older. They were about the same height, which surprised him. He had expected him to be taller.

"*Lo Dao*," Dad called him quietly.

Ye Ye nodded. He stuck his hand out, inviting Dad to shake it. They did, stiffly.

Then Dad turned to look at his mother, Ah Ngeen. It had been thirteen years since he had last seen her. Her face had grown rounder, wider. And her hair was cut short. He was surprised to see her wearing a T-shirt and slacks. He had imagined she would appear as she had in that photo, in a freshly pressed dress and high heels. Instead, she was dressed as though she were back in Jingweicun.

He was just about to greet her but Ye Ye cut him off.

"Did you have to tell them the watches were brand new? And why did you buy three of them?"

The face he'd seen from behind the glass wall was back. Ye Ye looked annoyed. That was why he'd been in the customs office—they were making him pay the duty on the watches. Dad had no idea. He also had no idea that when Ye Ye had originally asked for two watches, he'd already intended to give Dad one as a gift.

"Why didn't you just tell them you had worn them before?" Then he started lecturing him about the fancy camera and the brand new leather coat, the extravagances he had bought for himself with Ye Ye's money.

As he recounted this, Dad began to laugh. "The first time I met my dad—and he was scolding me."

• • • • • • •

They walked out together, the four of them, into the parking lot. They stopped next to a mustard yellow station wagon.

"This is yours?" Dad asked in disbelief. Ye Ye nodded and told him to get in.

Nobody he knew owned a car back in China. Only government officials and taxi drivers. They drove through Richmond, through the large swaths of farmland he'd seen from the airplane. It didn't look that different from Jingweicun, except the houses were huge and spread out between giant pieces of land.

Before long, they were on the Knight Street Bridge, which would take them into Vancouver. He had never seen so many lanes of traffic before. It was dizzying, even busier than what he'd seen in Hong Kong. Along the way, Great-Aunt asked most of the questions. She asked him about relatives back in Jingweicun, how everyone was doing. When she ran out of questions about the village, she asked about his travels, whether he'd eaten on the plane, and whether the plane ride had been comfortable.

About thirty minutes later, they pulled up next to a two-storey, dark beige house on McSpadden Avenue. It was just off Commercial Drive, an area populated mostly with Italian and Portuguese immigrants. The house they parked in front of was finished with clapboard, and had a porch and a tidy front yard with grass.

Dad couldn't believe this was their house. Back in Guangzhou, Ah Gong had always talked about wanting to own a house. In China, it had been an impossible dream.

They walked through the front door, Dad lugging his suitcase beside him. They were greeted with a crush of voices. Inside, there were dozens of people. Some of them looked vaguely familiar. Others he didn't think he'd met before. "These are all your relatives and our friends," Ah Ngeen told him. Great-Aunt's kids and her husband were all there. And Ms. Lee, who owned a farm out in Delta, was there with her kids. Mr. Ma, a friend of Ye Ye's, who liked to tell people's fortunes. Dad greeted them one by one, forgetting most of their names almost instantly.

Then he was led in front of a small shrine in the kitchen— a wood placard blessing the home, a couple of oranges to serve as an offering and a bowl filled with rice and the remnants of incense sticks. "It's time to *Bai sun,*" Ye Ye said. Pay respects to our ancestors. It wasn't like China, where they could visit the burial plot just a short walk from the house. Here, they'd had to build a shrine. One by one, they took turns bowing in front of it. Dad held the incense, rolling the red sticks between his index fingers and thumbs, before holding them in front of his forehead. He closed his eyes and paused a few seconds, thinking about Jingweicun. The thick smell of sandalwood filled the house.

Then it was time to eat. Ah Ngeen and the female relatives had spent the entire morning cooking a feast to welcome him to his new home. He looked at the table laid in front of him. There was a chicken, roast pork and plate after plate covered with vegetables. He glanced now at the kitchen counter. There was still more food there—extra dishes they didn't have room for on the table.

Afterward, Ah Ngeen and Ye Ye showed him around the house. They took him upstairs, where there were two bedrooms and a bathroom. "Janice and Jennie sleep here," said

Ah Ngeen, pointing to one of the rooms. His sisters. "They're still at school," she said.

Then they took him downstairs to the basement. Ye Ye had spent weeks building this room, Ah Ngeen told him. She pointed to the single bed and the wooden desk. He had built the furniture too, she said, pointing at Ye Ye. "This will be your room," she said.

Dad nodded. He had never had his own room before, but he didn't want to let on his surprise. He'd been so overwhelmed by the car, and the house, and the city. He didn't want them to think he was a bumpkin. They left him as he put his suitcase on the floor and began to unpack.

As he was folding his sweaters, he heard a commotion from upstairs. The door slamming shut and then footsteps running. A few moments later, a small head peeked out from behind the doorway. Then another. Both girls had tanned skin, blunt bangs and long, straight black hair.

They stared curiously at him. He stared back. He didn't know it, but the two girls, who were just nine and seven, had only been told a few weeks earlier that he would be coming. Until that point, they hadn't even known they had a brother.

After a few seconds of staring, he finally put his hand up and tried greeting them with their Chinese names. But he was met with blank faces. They didn't seem to understand him. Ah Ngeen had warned him earlier that they spoke mostly English.

He didn't know what else to do, so he just smiled. The two girls smiled back. No one seemed to know what to say or do. Finally, the two girls turned on their heels and ran away.

That night, Dad lay in his bed, staring up at the ceiling. The bed felt hard against his back, but that wasn't what was keeping him up.

For years, he had dreamed about this day, about coming to this new country. He had imagined himself here, living under one roof with his parents and sisters. The past few months and weeks had been occupied with planning, filling out paperwork and gathering documents. And for the past week he'd only thought about getting here. Boarding the train, then plane, to arrive in this new place.

After all of that, he was finally here. He was under the same roof as Ah Ngeen and Ye Ye. They'd all had dinner together, talking and eating around one table just as he'd imagined. What they hadn't talked about was the years they'd been separated, or why. He wondered how much they even wanted him here. He thought about the blank faces on the two girls—his sisters who hadn't even known he existed.

CHAPTER THIRTEEN

Nackawic, NB.

Spring 2016

ON ABOUT HOUR five of an eight-hour drive from Quebec
City to Moncton, I found myself drifting off, thumbing
absently around on my phone. By this point, we had been on
the road for over a week. The long drives—the blur of the
highway signs, the Tim Hortonses, the same five songs that
kept playing on the radio—were starting to grow tiresome. I
glanced over at Anthony, who had a glazed expression on his
face. I could tell he was tired. I knew I was.

"Maybe we should stop in a town," I suggested. "Maybe
check out a Chinese restaurant in one of them." There was
a town coming up called Nackawic with a restaurant. It was
called Saigon's Garden after the former name of the capital of
Vietnam. But according to Google, it was a Chinese restaurant
and, going by its ratings, it was a good one. So we exited off
the Trans-Canada Highway, taking the Route 105 Bridge over
the river and into the town.

After about twenty minutes of weaving around Nackawic,

along the Saint John riverbank, past a pulp mill and the "world's largest axe" statue, I started to grow suspicious. Our GPS was taking us down a rural road, past mostly wooded areas. We pulled the car over and looked at the GPS map more closely. The road would continue like this for as far as we could see. It didn't look right.

I dialled Saigon's Garden on my phone. A very young-sounding woman picked up.

I asked for the address of the restaurant.

The girl hesitated. She excused herself, saying she had to go look it up.

It occurred to me that, in a town of fewer than a thousand people, customers rarely needed to know the address of the place. They just knew where it was. A few minutes later, she returned to the phone. The address online was wrong. I wondered how long it had been that way without anyone having ever noticed.

We turned around, back toward the highway, and then turned onto a rural road, driving a few more minutes before pulling up next to a squat-looking brick building with a dusty blue roof. Except for a small sign above the window, there was no indication that it was a restaurant and not, say, an auto parts shop. Down the road was a pharmacy and an old farmhouse. Otherwise it was surrounded by shrub and forest.

We pulled open the glass door to find a cheerful-looking sign above the counter. "Welcome to Saigon's Garden." There was a dining room to the left.

The young woman we'd spoken with on the phone was behind the counter, and I ordered a couple of spring rolls and egg rolls. By this point, I had given up on eating a full meal at every restaurant we visited. We could only eat so many Cantonese chow meins, and many of our visits took place between meal times. Instead, I had taken to ordering spring rolls and egg rolls at every restaurant we visited. This way, we were at least ordering something. And if they ended up going to waste, at least it was only a little bit of food.

Truthfully, we probably could have chosen just one of the two—either egg rolls or spring rolls. But by this point in the trip, I still couldn't keep track of which was which. I knew I liked one better than the other, but it was embarrassing having to keep asking, over and over, which was which.

The woman seated us in the dimly lit dining room. The room was modestly decorated, save for a few pieces of Vietnamese art on the wall. There was one other table occupied by three middle-aged customers wearing ski jackets who gave us curious looks. When the woman returned with our water, I asked if the owner was around.

About ten minutes later, a young man wearing a puffy vest and glasses appeared at our table. He was tall, with short, spiky hair. He introduced himself as Gen Le, then apologized for keeping us waiting. He'd just arrived at the restaurant about half an hour earlier, he said, so the kitchen was backed up with orders.

"Where were you coming from?" I asked.

"School," he said.

The answer caught me off guard. I asked how old he was.

"Twenty-two."

Each morning, he would wake up and drive the forty-five

minutes to New Brunswick Community College in Fredericton, where he studies accounting, he explained. From eight-thirty in the morning until about three-thirty every afternoon, he had class. After class, he'd drive straight back to Nackawic, where he lived with his sister and parents. It was his sister and him who ran the restaurant. By about four p.m, four-thirty at the latest, he was usually back at the restaurant working.

Then once the restaurant closed around eight, he'd go home to do his homework. From Monday to Friday, week after week, this was his routine.

He must have noticed my awed expression because he added, quickly, "I've gotten used to it." He had a gentle giant quality to him—tall and broad-shouldered, with an impish smile and soft-spoken manner. He spoke with a slight lisp.

His parents had taken over this restaurant in 2006, he explained. His family is ethnically Vietnamese, but figured it made more sense to run a Chinese restaurant than a Vietnamese one. In a town like Nackawic, he said, "nobody knows what Vietnamese food is." But his parents have gotten older. And now his dad is sick.

So he and his sister decided to take over the family business. The two of them support their parents. Eventually, once he's finished school, they might shut down the restaurant. But for now, it's what's supporting the family.

When he was finished explaining to me his daily schedule I gently interrupted him.

"You know this isn't a normal life for a twenty-two-year-old, right?"

He just smiled. He's glad to be able to do it.

"I'm fine with it," he said. "Keeping myself busy—I've gotten used to it."

. . . .

As we left Saigon's Garden, I couldn't stop thinking about my conversation with Mr. Le. He seemed genuinely content. It brought to mind a young woman I'd met over a decade ago, Gah-Ning Tang.

At the time, I had been working on a magazine story about the children's author Robert Munsch. In my reporting, I had interviewed Ms. Tang, who had been friends with Mr. Munsch since she was a kid. Decades earlier, at the age of eight, she had written him a letter from her home in Hearst, a tiny logging town in Northern Ontario. In the letter, she had enclosed a hand-drawn picture of herself holding a cluster of balloons lifting her up and away. The picture charmed the writer and eventually inspired his book *Where Is Gah-Ning?* about a little girl who uses balloons to escape her tiny town.

Like Mr. Le, Ms. Tang, too, had grown up in a Chinese restaurant. The restaurant was the reason her family was in Hearst. It was the reason she was so eager to leave, whether it was by car, a train or a bunch of balloons. Mr. Le had told me he didn't mind spending all of his time at the restaurant. But I remembered that for Ms. Tang, that hadn't been the case. She and I were about the same age and had stayed in touch over the years. So I called her up.

"I really didn't like being in the restaurant," she told me. Her family lived in the same building as the restaurant, so there was no way of escaping the family business. The brick building on George Street in downtown Hearst housed the King's Cafe on the main floor. And in the basement apartment was where Ms. Tang lived with her parents and sister.

There was no division, she said. Anytime they weren't doing homework or working on a school project, she and her sister were expected upstairs, to help out. "Our uncle joked that when you're tall enough to reach in the sink, you're old enough to do the dishes," she said. When they were little, helping out meant running up and downstairs for supplies—grabbing ingredients from the freezer and bringing them up to her dad in the kitchen upstairs. And when they were older, they would help with packing takeout or catering orders, and wait tables.

They weren't paid for their work. It was just expected. "My dad wanted us to learn that you're supposed to help your family," Ms. Tang said. She actually didn't mind the work itself. Sometimes she didn't mind the restaurant even.

She just wished her life wasn't so *different* from everyone else's around her. Her friends at school didn't have to work. They got to do whatever they wanted after school. They were allowed to go to sleepovers. They lived in houses.

When her friends slept in on the weekends, they didn't have to wait until the breakfast rush was over before their dad could make them something to eat in the kitchen. Her friends were allowed to go to prom, they weren't told they had to work instead (her uncle later intervened, and she was allowed to go). And her friends didn't spend evenings scrubbing the restaurant bathroom because someone had drawn graffiti on the wall.

"I fought with [my parents] a lot. I was like, 'Why can't I have a normal childhood? Why did we have to end up in a restaurant? Why can't we just live in a house?'"

But now that she's grown older and moved out on her own to Toronto, her views have changed. The experience taught her a good work ethic, she thinks. And even though her parents were busy, having them upstairs meant they were always around if she really needed them. She also thinks that, by working at the restaurant, she was able to get to know them in a way that most kids don't—as colleagues and peers, as opposed to simply parents.

"As much as I had a list of things to hate," she said, "I still like our family's story."

Vancouver, BC.

1974-75

IN A CLASSROOM inside the beige-brick Britannia Second-
ary School in East Vancouver, the students sat in neat rows.
It was night school, Introduction to English, and the teacher
was going around the room one by one, asking Dad and the
other students where they were from. There were students from
Fiji, Peru and Korea, all of them newcomers. A few others
were Chinese. Some were from Guangdong and others from
Hong Kong.

"What's your name?" the instructor asked Dad in English.

He replied in Cantonese, "Hui Yam Hung."

"Do you have an English name?"

He said he didn't.

The teacher scrunched his brow, then thought for a few
seconds.

"My sisters have English names," Dad added. "Jennie and
Janice."

The teacher nodded thoughtfully.

"Well, why don't I give you a J-name too, then?" he asked. "How about we call you—Johnny?"

Dad thought about it. English names weren't like Chinese names, he had learned. They didn't have to be filled with meaning or poetry. Johnny was a name like any other.

"Johnny," he repeated. "Johnny. I am Johnny." He nodded his head, and the teacher printed the name out for him in a notebook.

• • • • • • •

The original plan had been for Dad to work with Ye Ye on his construction projects. But within a few weeks of working together, it became clear to Dad that he'd have to find another job.

Since that first meeting at the airport, things had remained tense between the two of them. Both men were quiet, and stubborn—accustomed to doing things their own way and unchallenged. Neither one was the type to initiate conversation, or even make small talk. They could barely figure out how to act around one another, never mind work together.

At work, Ye Ye was temperamental, quick to berate Dad for any mistake. In response, Dad would quietly fume. After half a year, and at the end of one particularly combative day, Dad decided he'd had enough. There was no way he could keep working with Ye Ye. But what else was there?

In China, where everything was laid out for him, he'd found his lack of choices suffocating. But now he realized it had

152

at least been a safety net. Ye Ye and Ah Ngeen were able to provide for him, but only to a point.

At the end of English class one day, a government official came to assign the students to their co-op placements. This was a requirement for new immigrants like Dad. Sitting across from him, the official asked Dad what he wanted to do. Dad told the man that he had only a high school education and some basic English skills. All he knew was that he didn't want to keep working in construction.

The officer asked what he thought about restaurant work. Most of the Chinese immigrants were working in restaurants, the officer explained. Plus, hadn't he said he knew how to cook? It seemed like a no-brainer.

To Dad, a job was a job. If it got him out of working with Ye Ye, it was fine with him. He said yes.

• • • • • • •

Dad started at Gum Goon, "the Golden Crown," the next day. It was, at the time, the biggest and fanciest restaurant in Chinatown, near the Woodward's building. The restaurant took up both the second and third floor of the downtown building.

That morning, he rode up the escalator into the giant dining room, marvelling at the idea of an escalator *inside of a restaurant*. The second floor, where he was going to work, was the dim sum dining room. The third floor, decorated with elaborate dragons carved out of wood, was where the restaurant held weddings and banquets.

Dim sum was where most of the beginner cooks started. As soon as they handed him his apron, they had him stand to the side, watching as dozens of chefs and cooks rushed around, balancing tall stacks of steamers and heating up giant woks the size of small tables. It felt like chaos.

The kitchen itself was huge, divided into three sections. The first section was where steamed dishes were made, where trays of *har gow, siu mai* and braised ribs were stacked carefully. The second area was for stir-frying and deep-frying, where handfuls of *jian dui* were lowered carefully into hot oil. The last section was for barbecue: golden-yellow whole chickens, *char siu* with shiny, sticky red skin and crispy, brown roast duck.

All of the *si fus*—the chefs—stood on the same side of the room. Most of them had spent many years cooking in Hong Kong before Gum Goon had brought them here. Most of these men specialized in just one variation of cooking—barbecue, or stir-frying, or dim sum. With their sauce-splattered T-shirts and black-and-white checkered pants, these men were the only ones allowed to wield the wok paddle for the stir-fries, turn the barbecue in the hot oven or manage the deep-fryer baskets.

The head chef, who was in charge of the entire kitchen, worked the steamers. He kept a careful eye on the *har gow* and *siu mai*, the staples that marked the difference between mediocre and great dim sum restaurants. The shrimp filling for mediocre *har gow* was cloaked in thick, gummy wrappers that stuck to the teeth like pencil erasers. Great *har gow* had a translucent skin, thin enough to fold into eight or more pleats. Great *har gow* yielded pleasantly at the bite.

On the other side of the room, opposite the *si fus*, was everyone else: the prep cooks, the food runners and the dishwashers. This was where Dad worked.

In his first few weeks, he spent entire shifts running around, gathering ingredients for the chefs. *Si fu* would call out "*har gow*," and it was Dad's job to run and bring out more baskets. Or he'd call out the name of a stir-fry and Dad would run off to gather the onions and ginger and carrots in a bowl.

Within about a month, they began letting him assist with food preparation: chopping, cutting and washing ingredients for the *si fus*. For hours on end, it was his job to chop spareribs down into bite-sized pieces, which would later be steamed with black beans and garlic. Other days, he would cut up hundreds of chicken feet, careful that they were uniform in length, to cook evenly as *feng zhao*.

Once in a while, one of the *si fus* might offer some advice, telling Dad to defrost the meat longer before cutting, for example, to make it easier. But most didn't have the time or the patience.

The work was repetitive. And when the restaurant was busy, such as on Saturday or Sunday afternoons, it was hectic. But Dad enjoyed it. He liked working with his hands and being able to see the results of his work: the pile of spareribs he chopped growing larger and larger. He liked figuring out how to do things. He liked how, by the end of a shift, he would discover simple solutions that would make the next day easier.

He also loved tasting the food. Many of the dim sum dishes were new to him too. This was *restaurant* food, and his family had rarely eaten out in China. Even if he had, many of these dishes didn't even exist in Guangzhou, and certainly not in Jingweicun. These were Hong Kong dishes, created by the chefs who wore tall white hats and were trained to cook for British officials. Occasionally, when a *si fu* had extra of something, or a dish that hadn't come out quite right, he'd set it aside for the kitchen staff. Dad would sidle over, popping a piece into his mouth. He catalogued the dishes and the flavours in his head.

As he reached the end of his six-month placement, he had a discussion with a former classmate from his English class, an older man in his forties. Mr. Chen was a *si fu*, sponsored by Nanking Restaurant on East Pender to come to Canada as a skilled immigrant. Dad told Mr. Chen about how he enjoyed his work at Gum Goon, but worried about the potential for advancement. All of the *si fus* at Gum Goon were relatively young and nowhere near retirement. If Dad wanted to move up in that kitchen, he would have a long wait ahead of him.

"Why don't you come work for me?" Mr. Chen said.

So, once Dad's placement was over, he did.

Nanking was a much smaller restaurant. Unlike the lavish Gum Goon, this one had just a couple dozen tables. It was much more casual—a family-style restaurant. Officially, Dad was hired on as a dishwasher. But because the kitchen staff was so small (just Mr. Chen, two other cooks and Dad), he would pitch in with food prep too.

At Nanking, the specialty was Peking-style duck. Dad watched, mesmerized, as Mr. Chen would hang the birds vertically to dry before roasting. When they were done roasting, he'd finish the ducks, holding them up one by one while using a large ladle to pour hot oil over them. The hot oil would fry the skin, creating a perfect golden-brown crust. Dad tried his first bite. The skin was thin and crispy. The meat inside tender and juicy. Hoisin added a hint of sweetness. It sent his head spinning.

All that time growing up, he had focused solely on the functional aspect of food. Food was survival. All he thought about was: Is there enough to eat, and how can I maximize what have? But at Gum Goon and now at Nanking, he was learning an entirely different world. There were flavours and ingredients, he discovered, that could set his heart racing. He was amazed at how, underneath all the chaos of the kitchen— the shouting, the boorishness of the *si fus* and the painstaking, obsessive efforts—everyone and everything was devoted solely to the *pleasure* of food.

A few weeks after Dad started at Nanking, Mr. Chen turned to him and asked him to make that night's staff meal. Every night after service, the kitchen cooks and waitresses ate together in the dining room. Simple, family-style meals: steamed vegetables, maybe a meat stir-fry and white rice. This was his chance to cook a meal from start to finish. And he could make anything he liked, Mr. Chen said.

So that night, Dad approached the wok nervously. In his hands he held a small bowl of thinly sliced beef that he had marinated with soy sauce, oyster sauce, sesame oil and corn-starch. He poured into the wok a little bit of oil and waited. After a few moments, he held his fingers under the faucet, then shook the water off above the wok, the way he'd seen the *si fus* do.

The oil hissed and sizzled. It was hot.

Into the hot wok, he dropped the beef mixture. Another loud hiss. He used the wok paddle to separate the slices. All the while, he kept a close eye on the flame below, careful not to let anything burn or overcook. *Tai foh,* just as he had learned to do all those years ago. As soon as he saw the edges of the beef turn from bright red to brown, he flipped them carefully, one by one. With the beef ready, he'd turn his focus to the vegetables. Into the same wok, he dropped the *gai lan,* adding a bit of water before covering it to steam.

He carefully arranged the bright green vegetables onto a clean plate. Then he scooped the beef on top. *Gai lan* with beef. He'd watched Mr. Chen make this dish a hundred times by now, and was anxious to try it himself.

Mr. Chen and the other cooks ate thoughtfully. Mr. Chen gave Dad some pointers. A little less cornstarch, he said. "See how these pieces are stuck together?" he said, poking at the beef with his chopsticks.

"But overall," he said, "not bad."

Not bad, Dad thought. That meant it could be better.

From then on, he kept a close eye on Mr. Chen and the other cooks around him. Each night, the staff meal remained his responsibility. And each night, Mr. Chen would offer his critiques. Too salty. Too sweet. Not enough *wok hay.* Dad took note of Mr. Chen's critiques, going over them in his head each night before bed.

Add more soy next time.

Wait until the wok gets hotter before adding the meat.

Steam for twelve minutes, not ten.

It can still get better.

Moncton, NB.

Spring 2016

I T WAS NEARLY ten p.m. by the time Anthony and I finally arrived in Moncton.

We hadn't yet eaten, so I searched to see what was around. The usual chain restaurants popped up first, Swiss Chalet and Harvey's and the like. There were some gastropubs and bistros too, but after an almost full day on the road, the last thing we wanted was to sit for an hour-long meal.

I kept searching until one of the results caught my eye. "Korean Restaurant/Acadia Pizza & Donair," it said. It was as if the owners had read both of our minds. For the past two days, Anthony had been talking about wanting a "proper, east-coast donair." The sweet, sticky white donair sauce I found so repulsive he found delicious. "Sweet meat?" I asked, and he nodded back with wide eyes that said, *Yes, please!* Meanwhile at that point, I was craving Korean food—or any Asian food that wasn't Chinese, at that point.

We drove up to the restaurant, a small white building with

a red roof located on a quiet sleepy stretch in the Moncton suburb of Dieppe. The restaurant was tiny. We could see the entire dining room without turning our heads. Posted on the walls and behind the counter were the menus. There were a few of them. One menu was Korean, with dishes like *japchae* and *ramyun*. And then there was a menu with traditional maritime dishes like the donair. And then there were hybrids.

Behind the counter, a middle-aged Korean man with neatly styled hair and an apron tied around his waist greeted us with a smile. He was friendly and answered our questions about the menu. "*Bulgogi* pizza," he explained. "It's *bulgogi*—sweet-marinated beef—tomato sauce and cheese."

It was a breed of pizza that had recently become popular in Korea. These were pizzas that had little to do with their Italian ancestors, often topped with traditional Korean ingredients like *gochujang*. Others blended in American ingredients, like hash browns or nacho chips. I had heard that Korean pizza was beginning to appear in cities with large Korean populations, like Los Angeles. But never would I have imagined finding it in a sleepy place like Dieppe.

Later, when he brought over my steaming bowl of spicy *ramyun*, we introduced ourselves.

He introduced himself as Jae Chong. He gestured toward the kitchen, where a middle-aged woman was working. "My wife, Eun-jung Lee," he added.

He said there'd been a small boom in Moncton's Korean population about a decade earlier, when local business groups undertook recruitment efforts in the hope that new immigrants might stimulate the local economy. Between 2006 and

2011, the Korean population in Moncton increased from 65 to about 550. Many of those newcomers became his customers. Plus, he added, there were some locals in Dieppe who loved Korean food, such as the ones who had travelled to Korea to teach English.

But for those who had never had Korean food before, dishes like *bulgogi* pizza were designed as a way of introducing them to Korean flavours. It was like chop suey, but Korean.

I asked him how they'd wound up in Canada, and he explained how he and his wife moved to Canada for the sake of their two sons, who were both studying music. They had initially moved to Fredericton, but later came to Moncton in order to be closer to their sons' music teachers. The restaurant helped pay for the music lessons. He pointed to the wall, at a poster advertising a classical music concert. "My son," he said proudly.

As we spoke, I thought about how, the farther we travelled and the more restaurants we visited, the more I began to see how loosely the term "Chinese restaurant" might be applied.

There were the restaurants that just happened to be run by Chinese: cafes and steakhouses and "Western restaurants." Sometimes they had spring rolls and chicken balls tossed onto their menu alongside the steaks and sandwiches. But not always.

Then there were chop suey restaurants, dozens of which we'd already visited. Some of them hadn't even been run by Chinese people, like Lan Huynh, the Vietnamese woman selling "Chinese pierogis" in Glendon, or Mr. Le in Nackawic.

I remembered how Henry Yu at UBC had emphasized *families*, and said to me that the term "Chinese restaurant" might be better defined by the labour—the family networks that ran them, rather than the cuisine.

In his view, it was the "family restaurant" system that made these places Chinese. It was a business model dependent on uncles and aunts and cousins and grandparents all pitching in. It was the system described by Mr. Choy in Stony Plain and Ms. Tang in Hearst of the kid in the back of the restaurant, washing dishes between homework. It was the template we'd seen all along our trip.

Professor Yu had also mentioned how many of the new Chinese immigrants in larger cities were opening non-Chinese restaurants. It was a trend I'd seen in Vancouver and Toronto— how so many new sushi restaurants, or Thai restaurants, or pho restaurants were actually run by Chinese families. These too, he said, might be considered "Chinese restaurants." After all, it was all the same model—just different food.

Now, as I finished the last bites of my *ramyun*, I wondered whether this little restaurant in Dieppe might fit that definition too. That, as Professor Yu had pointed out, maybe a "Chinese restaurant" really wasn't about the food or ethnicity at all. Instead, it was all about the families. The *family restaurant*.

Ms. Lee came over with a plate covered with aluminum foil. The *bulgogi* pizza was finally ready. Anthony picked up a slice, then took a large bite. Long strings of cheese stretched from the pie to his mouth. "It's different, eh?" Mr. Chong said, chuckling. "It's different!"

Abbotsford, BC.

1976-77

O N A CLEAR day, you can see from the window in my parents' living room all the way across Burnaby. Their house is on the top of a hill and faces south, overlooking the tiny houses in neat rows and skyscraper condos in the distance. But on one grey January day, all of those neighbourhoods were clouded over, disappearing behind a thick veil of fog. Still, Dad sat next to the window, staring out from his usual spot on the couch.

For the past few weeks, he'd been getting worse. His naps were getting longer. He was spending almost all of his time on the couch. He skipped a Saturday hike with his friends. Even indoors, he wore a toque and puffy vest on top of a fleece sweater to stay warm. I'd offer to cook and he'd accept a little too eagerly. On this day especially, he was cranky and tired. All of us were. We'd driven out to the hospital that morning for another one of his appointments. More bad news.

Mom and I decided to leave him be. We were flipping

through old photos: mostly wedding photos and pictures of their first years of marriage.

They had met in ESL class, where Mom had caught Dad's attention. Unlike the other girls in class who were shy and quiet, she was loud and talkative. She had short hair, styled in a pixie cut like the Hong Kong starlets. Her name was Siu Hung, or "Little Red." But she hated the name. By coincidence, it happened to be a name commonly used in Chinese movies and television shows for prostitutes. She also resented the implication that there was anything small about her.

In class, Mom was often the first to raise her hand when the instructor asked questions. Only later did the instructor realize it was because she had been placed in a beginner class by mistake. She had grown up in Hong Kong and studied English throughout her schooling. But for whatever reason, during her assessment, she had had a bout of uncharacteristic shyness. And so she wound up stuck with the rest of the beginners, relearning her ABCs and 123s.

One day after class, she marched up to Dad. She was organizing a class outing.

"Hey, are you coming to Queen Elizabeth Park with us this weekend?"

Dad looked at the woman, with her pixie cut and sharp eyes.

"You should come," she said. He did, and they wound up spending the afternoon together. Two years later, they were married.

The photos were carefully arranged in albums bound in emerald Thai silk or bright fuchsia floral patterns.

The pictures showed Mom flanked by her bridesmaids,

getting ready for their wedding at St. Francis Xavier in Chinatown. She wore a Victorian lace gown and a white Eliza Doolittle hat over her mushroom-cut hair. Dad posed next to her, dressed in a powder-yellow tux with a bow tie. It seemed like an odd choice, considering the only sartorial flourishes he took these days were the hats he collected in his travels.

"Why yellow?" I said, turning to my mom.

It was a rental, she said, and a popular colour at the time. It seemed as good an explanation as any.

We flipped through the pictures, one by one. There was a sepia-kissed image of Po Po brushing Mom's hair in the traditional Chinese pre-wedding ceremony. Mom had done the same for me at my wedding—insisting that I buy new pajamas, because old pajamas would bring bad luck to the marriage. With each stroke of the hair brush, she counted aloud, then offered a blessing.

One. A marriage that lasts a lifetime.

Two. A happy and harmonious partnership.

Three. A home full of children and grandchildren.

Four. A marriage that grows into old age.

There was a picture of my aunts serving as bridesmaids, dressed in pastel gowns with their bangs neatly curled. My uncles wearing boutonnieres of red carnations and baby's breath. They all looked so young and full of energy.

Sitting in the living room now, Mom kept one eye on the pictures and another on Dad. By now, he had reclined his seat on the couch and was taking a nap. She gazed just slightly past the images, as if the people in the photos were strangers.

After the wedding, she said, she moved into the house with Ye Ye, Ah Ngeen, Jennie and Janice.

I asked what that was like.

She widened her eyes and shook her head.

"The first few months were hard," she said.

Dad still hadn't adjusted to living with Ye Ye and his new family. And though Dad and Ye Ye were no longer working together, they were still tense around one another. Adding my mother—a headstrong Hong Konger—into the mix further upset the household rhythm.

Small gestures that seemed perfectly normal to Mom seemed wasteful and frivolous to her new in-laws. Mom had grown up poor too. Po Po had raised her and her siblings in public housing in Hong Kong. From the time she was nine years old, Mom worked in a sweatshop making plastic flowers and beaded jewellery to help feed her brothers and sisters. But poor was relative. Mom was Hong Kong poor. Mainland China poor—Jingweicun poor—was a different level of desperation.

And now that Mom was in Vancouver, making decent wages as a waitress at the Hyatt Regency downtown, she was anxious to explore her new life. One day not long after moving in, she bought giant pots of rich golden chrysanthemums. She wanted to plant them outside the front door, something pretty to decorate her new home. But Ah Ngeen scolded her. To her, the flowers were a waste of time and money.

Another day, Mom took Jennie and Janice downtown to taste pizza for the first time. There were so many new foods in Vancouver, and she was curious to try them all. They bit into the hot slices, surprised by the tangy, sweet tomato sauce and the crunch of the crust. Mom thought it was tasty, even if Jennie and Janice weren't won over. When they got home, Ah Ngeen was irritated that Mom had fed the girls these foreign foods.

"They need rice!" she said with a loud sigh. She'd have to feed them again.

Tensions between Dad and Ye Ye, meanwhile, kept boiling over. Over the dinner table or in the hallway on the way to the bathroom, they'd squabble. Ye Ye didn't understand why Dad didn't follow his example.

"Why bother with English school?"

"Why aren't you working with me in construction?"

"Why are you wasting time in restaurants?"

Dad was still at the Nanking. He was getting paid $1.25 an hour—roughly $10 each day, or $200 each month. He wasn't sure what the older cooks or Mr. Chen were earning, but he suspected it wasn't much more than him. On the other hand, he knew that the restaurant's owner was doing very well, owning properties and businesses all over Chinatown.

He knew he'd only get so far working for others.

One day, Dad returned home excited. He told Mom about a convenience store he'd seen up for sale near the corner of Macdonald and Broadway, in the Kitsilano neighbourhood. Some of their friends owned convenience stores and seemed to be doing well with them. They could take over this one and run it. It would be their own business. Mom trekked out with him to see it. The shop was in a great location, close to the beach and out toward a university.

But the owners wanted forty thousand dollars for the business. And that didn't include the cost of all the inventory Mom and Dad would have to buy upfront. They didn't have anywhere near that kind of money. They looked at lesser locations. But even so, the cost to stock the business with supplies seemed insurmountable.

So their minds turned to restaurants. It was a business they already knew, and without the same upfront costs. Like Dad, Mom had been assigned by immigration officials to restaurant work. She spoke English, so they had placed her at the Hyatt. Between the two of them, they already knew how to run both the front and back of house.

They looked at a few available spaces in Vancouver. Each night, Dad would pull out his calculator. He'd sketch out on pieces of grid paper the cost of each restaurant, the monthly rent and projected income. And he'd look at their meagre savings and what they thought they'd be able to borrow from the banks. Each time, he'd look up at Mom, brow furrowed. The numbers didn't add up.

Then Uncle Zachary came to them with news about a Chinese restaurant for sale, priced within their budget. The only problem was that the restaurant wasn't in Vancouver. It wasn't even in one of the closer suburbs, such as Burnaby or Richmond. The restaurant was about an hour outside of Vancouver, in a town called Abbotsford—a town they had never heard of.

Abbotsford. When they looked at it on the map, it seemed so far. It would mean leaving behind all their family and friends, for a place they knew nothing about.

At the same time, it seemed to present a number of opportunities. It was affordable. And, from what they could tell, there wouldn't be much competition in a place like Abbotsford.

As an added bonus, working an hour away meant they had an excuse to move out of Ye Ye's house.

• • • • • • • •

About a week later, Uncle Zachary drove Dad and Mom out to Abbotsford to see the restaurant for themselves. It was the first time any of them had seen the town. When they took the exit off the highway, they were surprised to find long stretches of farmland. It reminded Dad of Jingweicun.

Even in the town centre, the buildings were no more than two or three storeys. They lined only the handful of main roads. On South Fraser Way, what looked to be the main road, Uncle Zachary slowed his car to a stop, parking next to a white building. It was the Legion Hall, a stucco building with red trim. The restaurant was inside the hall.

Mom and Dad gawked from the car. The windows were framed with dusty-looking curtains. The sign on the side of the building was sparse. "Legion" was written in black cursive and "Restaurant" in thick block letters. A Pepsi sign hung to the right, above the entrance.

The signs and building looked faded and dated. The "Open" sign on the door looked hand-drawn.

I interrupted Mom as she spoke. It occurred to me that I'd only ever seen a couple photos of the Legion, but never one of the exterior. From his spot on the couch, Dad stirred. We thought he'd been sleeping, but apparently he'd been listening the entire time.

He yawned, then stood up. A few minutes later, he returned with a photo album. He pointed to a picture and handed it to me.

"Here," he said.

I looked at the picture. It was just as they'd described: a dusty-looking building and a faded sign. But something caught my attention when I looked at the restaurant's sign.

The word "Legion," was scrawled in black cursive, just as Mom had said. Beside it was the word "Restaurant" in big block letters. But it was the words underneath that caught my eye.

"CANADIAN AND CHINISE CUISINE," the sign read.

I looked at the words again, spelling the letters out loud, to be sure.

"C-H-I-N-I-S-E."

I looked from the photo, up to my dad, then back at the photo.

"Dad," I said, handing him back the photo. "Do you notice anything strange about the sign?"

He looked at the photo, leaning in close to read the letters.

"Canadian and Chinese Cuisine," he said. "What's wrong?"

"You don't notice anything strange about the spelling?"

"Chinese Cuisine," he repeated. "C-H-I-N-I." His voice dropped. "Oh."

He was silent for a moment. He shook his head back and forth, like he couldn't believe it.

But then his chest began to heave up and down. His shoulders were shaking. He was laughing.

"Frances," he said, passing the picture to her. He was gasping for air now. "Frances, look."

Once she realized what he was pointing at, she grimaced. She didn't find it as funny as he did. But that seemed to make him laugh even harder.

He pulled his glasses off his face, cackling with his entire body.

"We had no idea!" he said. "The people in Abbotsford must have laughed and laughed. *And we had no idea!*"

• • • • • • •

Staring from the car window that day, Dad wasn't looking at the dirty windows or the chipped paint. Instead, he saw the library next door. And on the other side, the office for an insurance company. Across the street, construction crews were building what looked like a new strip plaza. Next to him, he saw a steady flow of traffic, what seemed to be a reasonably busy street. What he saw were customers. Potential.

Less than a month later, he and Mom signed the contract to purchase the restaurant.

They paid twenty-four thousand dollars for the business. Of that, thirteen thousand came from their own savings. One thousand came as a loan from one of Dad's friends, a young man named Hon Ming Woo, whose mother had been one of the eight people in the room with Dad at the Guangzhou immigration office. The rest came from the bank.

Ye Ye disapproved of the decision. He had worked hard for decades to build a life in Vancouver. He and Ah Ngeen had

scrimped and saved and sacrificed to buy a house, a car—
unimaginable luxuries compared to their lives back in China.
They'd brought Dad to Canada to share in it. They thought
they were giving him opportunities they'd never had. And
now Dad was turning his back on it all and moving to a small
town nobody had ever heard of.

There was a fight, and then a declaration.

"If you move out," Ye Ye told them, "you're not welcome
back."

Glace Bay, NS.

Spring 2016

A s soon as Anthony and I crossed the New Brunswick–
Nova Scotia border, driving over the Missaguash River,
fat, lazy snowflakes began dropping down onto our windshield,
melting instantly onto the glass.

It got heavier as we drove deeper into the province. By the
time we reached Truro to fill up on gas, it was a blizzard.

The original plan had been to drive at a leisurely pace toward
Sydney. There, on the eastern tip of the province, we had
a hotel room booked for the night. It should have been a
straightforward, five-hour drive, leaving lots of time to pop
into Chinese restaurants along the way. But because of the
snow, traffic on the highway had slowed to half speed. And
when snow turned to blizzard and it became difficult to see the
road, traffic slowed right down to a crawl. One after another,
we inched along the highway, each car following the next
faithfully into the fog.

Anthony glanced nervously at the GPS. He muttered under

his breath, "It's still 160 kilometres to Cape Breton Island." From there, he said, it would be another 130 kilometres to Sydney.

"Even if we drive straight to Sydney, at this speed it'll be late by the time we get there," Anthony said. He was nervous about driving in this weather in the dark. "These tires," he said, "they're basically just painted on."

We opted to be safe, abandoning our plans to make any stops.

It was already dark by the time we approached the Canso Canal Bridge, a narrow swing bridge that would take us onto Cape Breton Island.

For several hours, we'd been reasonably lucky. A giant tractor-trailer had been right ahead of us, carving fresh tracks into the snow for our tiny Fiat to follow. For those hours, the truck had been our guide. But just as we made our way toward the causeway, the trailer turned off the road toward a gas station. I swung around to look at the gas station. Several other trucks were parked there too. The road leading onto the bridge was empty.

"Is the road shut down?" I asked.

"There's no sign or anything," Anthony said. "It doesn't look like it."

His fingers were clamped around the steering wheel, his focus entirely on the road. We'd already passed the gas station. There was no choice but to drive forward.

We drove slowly, warily, onto the bridge.

About halfway across, a loud crash came from beneath us and I let out a small yelp. The storm waves were crashing up against the side of the bridge. Sheets of water sloshed up and over our car. Anthony just kept driving, stone-faced, keeping a tight grip on the wheel.

We drove onto the island and into total darkness. The lights were out. The storm must have caused a power outage. Between the blowing snow and near pitch-dark, even the highway signs were impossible to make out. It felt like something out of a horror film.

Ahead of us, the road split. On the left, the road sloped upward and into darkness. On the right, the road also led into darkness.

Anthony shrugged and chose the road on the right.

We drove deeper and deeper into the dark, with only the headlights from our little Fiat lighting our way. Anything beyond the few glowing feet ahead of us was impossible to see. I could tell from Anthony's silence that he was as worried as I was.

I worried about getting stuck, in the tiny little car, in the middle of the road. I worried we'd get hit. Or worse, that we'd hit someone—or something. Between the snow and the darkness, it would be impossible to see a deer or a moose on the road. Our toy car was no match for a moose. Anthony drove with the hazard lights on, just to be safe.

"If there's a hotel or something, do you want to pull over?" he asked. Better to be safe than worry about the money we'd spent on a hotel in Sydney. I nodded, gratefully.

On my phone, I did a quick search and brightened when I saw there were a few options ahead.

"Over here, on our right, we should be approaching a motel."

He slowed to a crawl as we approached the foggy outline of a strip motel along the highway. But the sign was dark. The lights were out. The building was shuttered.

"I guess it's closed for the season."

A few minutes later, another motel just up the road. But again, the sign was out. The lights were out. My heart dropped. We tried this a few more times before we realized they were all closed. It was April, and technically still off-season. The entire island, it seemed, was closed.

So we kept driving, Anthony's knuckles clamped on the steering wheel. The giant knot growing higher and higher in my throat. All I could think about was that gas station back at the causeway. The bright lights and the warm coffee shop. The parked tractor-trailers and the truck drivers huddled together safely.

What did they know that we didn't?

About half an hour later, we spotted it. A haze of orange light, just off in the distance.

We kept driving and the light grew brighter. It was a snow-plow. We had no idea who the driver was or where they were going. It didn't matter. For the time being, that driver was the most important person in our world.

Anthony breathed in quickly and sped up, until we were nestled in the truck's glow. Safety.

· · · · · · ·

The next morning, we woke up in our warm hotel bed in Sydney. We felt fortunate to have arrived safely. And after a shower and night's sleep, we felt recharged. But, it turned out, the storm wasn't finished with us.

The reason for staying in Sydney was to catch the morning ferry to Newfoundland. But the snowstorm had delayed our sailing. Instead of setting out that morning, we would instead leave twelve hours later, at night. Suddenly we had an extra half-day to spend in Cape Breton.

Over breakfast, we plotted out our backup plan. The hotel's dining room overlooked the city's waterfront. Below us was a long boardwalk promenade and a few tens of metres away, what looked to be a giant violin, about eighteen metres tall. When the waitress wandered over, she explained. "It's the world's largest fiddle," she said, raising her eyebrows, as if to say, *Go figure.* She was new to Sydney.

We would have found it strange too, except we had already encountered a number of similar attractions so far on the trip. There was the world's largest dinosaur, back in Drumheller. Also in Alberta, we'd seen the "world's largest" pysanka—an impressively detailed nine-and-half-metre tall Ukrainian-style Easter egg. That one was made even more impressive by the fact that it could move, rotating in circles on its perch in Vegreville. Less impressive was the world's largest perogy in Glendon—a lumpy dumpling hoisted half-heartedly in the air with a giant fork.

In Shediac, New Brunswick, Anthony had taken photos of me posing excitedly next to the world's largest lobster. In Nackawic, I was less enthusiastic about taking photos of the axe.

The attractions didn't just stop at the "world's largest." There was a giant Canada goose in Wawa, ON (the largest in Canada). And in White River, ON (the town where Lieutenant Harry Colebourn first encountered the little black bear he named Winnie—the bear that would inspire A.A. Milne to write his famous children's books), a statue of the little bear. Many of them had been built in an effort to draw greater tourism to the tiny towns. Like Vulcan and its Trekkie tourism, the tiny towns hoped to send a signal to drivers passing by on the highway. "We're here!" the attractions were built to say. "Turn off for a visit!"

After breakfast, we decided to get back in the car and drive around the island a bit. There was still a blanket of fresh snow covering most of the smaller roads and trails, so the obvious sightseeing options, such as the Cabot Trail, were off the table. Instead, we'd have to stick to the highways and cities. As we drove around, we passed a large Chinese restaurant called Huang's. It had a giant green, pagoda-style facade with yellow and red accents. The name "Huang's" was spelled out in huge, bright-red letters. It looked like what you might expect if Disney were to build a Chinese restaurant.

It reminded me of a similar-looking restaurant we had passed in Truro the day before. That restaurant, The Chow Family restaurant, also had a pagoda-like facade, painted in green, yellow and white. Its owners, too, had spelled out their restaurant's name in bright, cartoonish lettering. The more I thought about it, the more the two restaurants seemed eerily similar.

And then, a few minutes later, in Glace Bay, another Chinese restaurant. This one had a modest exterior, unlike the other two, but the name caught my eye. It was called Huang Family Restaurant. At this point, I was curious. Anthony parked outside the restaurant and walked over to the nearby Tim Hortons. Meanwhile, I made my way inside.

Inside, the waitress, a middle-aged white woman, seated me at a small table near the front with faded banquettes and paper printed placemats. At the back was a door leading to the kitchen.

There was a menu at the table I glanced at very quickly— chow mein and chicken balls.

The waitress turned around to head back to the bar. But before leaving, I noticed her eyeing me up and down. After a few moments, she returned with a laminated piece of paper. "This is for you—just in case," she said. I looked down. It was a different menu, written in Chinese. I looked at this one carefully. It was full of "authentic" Cantonese dishes. It was a second menu, meant for Chinese customers.

As I scanned the menu, a thin, middle-aged Chinese man with a salt-and-pepper mustache walked out from the kitchen and through the dining room. I heard him giving instructions to the waitress in English, something about his car needing repairs, before heading back toward the kitchen.

He was the restaurant owner, Allen Huang. I flagged him down and asked about the two menus. I'd seen two menus in Chinese restaurants in cities like Vancouver or Toronto before, but not in any of the smaller towns we'd visited on this road trip. He laughed and responded in Cantonese. When he'd first started this restaurant back in 1993, it had been a chop-suey-only restaurant. It was chicken balls and spring rolls and fried rice.

He was amazed at first by the food, he said. In China, everything he cooked was made from fresh. A chicken went from flapping its wings to steamed on a plate in less than half an hour. But here, people were fine with everything cooked from frozen, and even expected it. He gave me a look as if to say, *Can you believe it?*

He paused for a moment. The waitress was back to deliver news on the car repairs. There were delays. "No," he said firmly in English. "I need it by this afternoon. Tell them that."

He turned back to me. Glace Bay had been entirely white when he moved here. It was a former coal-mining town, and his was the only Chinese restaurant. So his business relied on chop suey and chow mein. But four years ago, that changed. An old junior high school in Glace Bay was converted into a private English-language school. Suddenly the town found itself playing host to hundreds of young people from all over the world who were looking to improve their English before heading to university in Sydney. Many of those foreign students were from China.

A few of them walked into Mr. Huang's restaurant expecting a taste of back home, but found themselves confused by the chop suey menu. Ever the entrepreneur, Mr. Huang realized these students were a market, so he created his second menu.

The waitress came back with good news on the car. Mr. Huang smiled and stood up to follow her.

Before he left, I remembered the over-the-top restaurants I'd spotted in Sydney—the cartoon-like decor and the brightly coloured signs. I asked him about them, whether the restaurant with the similar name, The Chow Family restaurant, and then the one that shared Chow's similar decor, Huang's Restaurant, were connected with his. He grinned.

Yes, the restaurants were connected, he said. He was the connection.

One of the first Chinese restaurants he worked at in Nova Scotia was The Chow Family restaurant. There, the owner at the time had taught him everything he knew. So when Mr. Huang opened his own Chinese restaurant years later, Huang's—that second, green-and-yellow pagoda-shaped restaurant we'd seen in Sydney—he applied what he'd learned, right down to the decor.

They're not *exactly* the same, he said. "It's just *almost* the same."

• • • • • • •

That night, we pulled into the Sydney ferry terminal to take the seven-hour, roughly 180-kilometre journey to Channel-Port aux Basques, NL.

After passing our reservation details to the woman in the ticket booth, she pointed us to the giant waiting area, where cars and trucks were parked in rows, ready to board. It was still early and many of the lanes were empty. But the lanes on the edges designated for trucks were full. The giant container trucks were lined up, one by one, filled with food, household goods, electronics—everything Newfoundlanders couldn't otherwise get on the island province.

The ferry service was run by a provincial crown corporation. Because of this, we'd expected it to look something like the ferries in BC, comfortable but bland. But once we boarded and surfaced onto the passenger deck, we were surprised to find a cabin decorated in bright pinks, purples and lime green. With the polished floors and thick, round columns, it was like a floating nightclub in the middle of the Gulf of St. Lawrence.

We walked across the rest of the main passenger level, taking in the cafés and cafeterias, a gift shop and multiple seating areas. Then we made our way downstairs.

The cabins, where we'd splurged on a sleeping bunk, were on a separate deck. The hallways were stark white, and the entrance to each cabin marked with a citrus-yellow door. We pulled open the door to ours. The entire cabin was maybe two and half metres wide, with a single bed on each side and a narrow walkway in between. There was a tiny bathroom in the corner with a toilet, a sink and a shower that was so small I couldn't possibly imagine using it.

As I tucked into my bed for the night, it reminded me of those summers working as a flight attendant. On the long-haul flights from Toronto to Hong Kong, we'd have our crew rest in bunks like these, tiny single beds. Here, as there, we buckled ourselves into bed with seatbelts before drifting off to the sound of safety announcements over the PA. The same waves that had terrified me and Anthony the night before were now rocking us gently to sleep.

I slept soundly that night, better than at any of the hotels we'd stayed at on previous nights.

But the next morning, Anthony wouldn't stop yawning over breakfast. I was surprised when he told me he hadn't been able to sleep. I asked him why.

"The rocking back and forth didn't bother you?"

"I didn't feel a thing," I said.

He raised his eyebrow. "I don't know, it was pretty bad."

A crew member—a middle-aged woman with blonde hair—walked over to clear the table next to ours.

Anthony turned to her. "Last night was a real rock polisher, eh?"

She turned to face him. "Excuse me?"

"The turbulence last night," he said. "A real rock polisher."

She looked at him and nodded vaguely.

He pressed on. "On a scale of one to ten, how bad would you say it was?"

She let out a small laugh that may have actually been a snort. She gave it a moment's thought.

"I'd say—about a two?"

Abbotsford, BC.

1977

M OM AND DAD found an apartment on Pauline Street, just around the corner from the Legion.

On their first day at the restaurant, they arrived at eight in the morning. The previous owner, a man named Mr. Cheung, greeted them. He'd agreed to stay on for the first week to show them the ropes. Mr. Cheung was just slightly older than Dad and wore his hair in a deep side part. He was originally from Hong Kong and had moved to Canada with his parents. But now they were elderly, and neither one spoke English. This meant he'd had to run the restaurant more or less on his own—taking orders and waiting tables out front, and then jumping into the kitchen to help with cooking too. He was burnt out and ready to go back to collecting a paycheque.

The first thing Mr. Cheung did was show Mom and Dad how to make coffee. This, he told them, was the most important thing he could teach them. It was 1976, before the proliferation of Starbucks or Tim Hortons. When people wanted coffee, they either made it at home or bought it at cafes like his. Many of the regulars would only be here for the coffee, Mr. Cheung told them.

He showed Dad the refrigerator, and how to organize the vegetables and meats on their own shelves. He also showed him his supplier lists, and how to put in his order at Fresh Pak, which would deliver all his fresh fruit and vegetables each week.

Then he walked Dad through the menu. He explained what a "special of the day" was—basically whatever he had extras of. And he explained why it was important to have a soup as a special every day. It meant getting rid of leftovers. Whatever happened to be in the refrigerator could be repackaged as soup. Leftover chicken became chicken noodle. Leftover turkey became cream of turkey. And leftover ham became split pea with ham.

Dad jotted down notes as quickly as he could while Mr. Cheung spoke. *Cream of turkey?* he thought to himself. *Split pea with ham?* They sounded so foreign.

When it was time for Mr. Cheung to teach Dad how to roast a turkey, he did a double-take at the bird that came out of the freezer. He had never seen or even heard of a turkey before. The smooth, hairless surface was wrapped in plastic. And it was huge. It looked nothing like the fresh chickens he had eaten growing up. Once roasted, Mr. Cheung taught him how to debone the bird: how to save the bones and giblets for soup and slice the breast for sandwiches.

"When people order a chicken sandwich, you can just give them turkey," Mr. Cheung instructed him. It would help to get rid of the turkey meat quicker, and customers wouldn't know the difference. "A turkey is just like a bigger chicken, right?"

Dad nodded *yes*, even if he wasn't sure he agreed.

Mr. Cheung taught him how to make hamburgers, then showed him what ketchup and mayonnaise were, and how much of each to use. He squirted a dime-sized amount of ketchup onto a spoon, and then a bit of mustard. He had Dad taste each, so he'd know the difference. "Ketchup—sweet," he said. "Mustard—sharp."

He worked his way down the menu, showing Dad how to make crispy fish and chips, sirloin steaks with a charred crust, bubbling tomato soup and veal cutlets. Most of these were foods Dad had never even tasted, let alone cooked. Dad tasted them, one by one, taking note of the flavours—sweet, salty, crispy, oily. They were so different from the ones he was used to. Mr. Cheung handed him a grilled cheese and ham sandwich, fresh off the grill. Dad took a bite. The melted cheese stretched into long strings. The cheese was piping hot and creamy. The ham was salty and sweet. He almost fell over.

Anytime Dad asked too many follow-up questions, or asked Mr. Cheung to repeat himself, the cook would only wave dismissively. "Most of the customers around here are farmers and labourers," he said. "They aren't gourmets."

"The most important thing is that it's cooked," Mr. Cheung told him. "As for the taste, well, there's salt and pepper on the table."

• • • • • • •

On the third day, Mr. Cheung switched to the other side of the menu. The "Chinese" menu.

"I already know how to cook Chinese food," Dad told Mr. Cheung. He'd spent the past year cooking it.

But this wasn't Chinese food, Mr. Cheung told him. This was *chop suey* Chinese. "The people here—they won't eat the food you cooked in Chinatown." He showed him sweet and sour pork, one of the most popular items on the Chinese menu. Sure, it was similar to *gu lou yuk*, a classic Cantonese dish, he explained, but there were key differences. He showed Dad how to make the sauce out of sugar, vinegar and ketchup, then build a batter out of cornstarch, egg and flour. "Be sure to make a thick batter to sop up more sauce," Mr. Cheung told him. Once the dish was done, Dad bit into the pork. It was crispy from the batter, and sweet and tangy all at the same time. The cubes of pineapple exploded between his teeth with salty, sweet juice. It was so sweet it tasted like candy.

"This is Chinese?" Dad asked.

Mr. Cheung nodded, grinning. "Chop suey Chinese."

Then Mr. Cheung taught him how to make chop suey. It was exactly what it sounded like, he explained.

Chop suey—*dsap sooy*. Assorted scraps. Bits and pieces. This and that.

In other words, whatever happened to be lying around.

The basic ingredients were always the same, Mr. Cheung said. There were always bean sprouts, onions and carrots. From there, you add whatever is available. For beef chop suey, some roast beef from the sandwiches. For chicken chop suey, the chicken, or turkey. And for vegetable chop suey, peppers and mushrooms, or whatever else had arrived in the Fresh Pak order that week.

Then soy sauce, sugar and salt.

"At the very end, always add a sprinkle of MSG. This is important," he said, turning to face Dad.

MSG, or monosodium glutamate, is the ubiquitous ingredient in every Chinese kitchen all over the world. It made everything taste better. But it was a controversial ingredient—a controversy that food historian Ian Mosby traces back to the 1960s, when a medical researcher posited in the *New England Journal of Medicine* that a variety of symptoms he was experiencing (numbness, weakness and heart palpitations) were due to MSG. This bolstered pre-existing suspicions of Chinese cuisine as "unclean" or "unsafe," and quickly became known as "Chinese restaurant syndrome," despite the fact that MSG is used in a variety of foods, including cheese and baby food. And though the idea of MSG-caused discomfort has since been dispelled by science, many mistakenly continue to believe the ingredient is harmful.

But not Mr. Cheung. He encouraged Dad to use the ingredient liberally, to make up for any shortcomings in flavour otherwise.

He repeated himself for emphasis. "Don't forget the MSG."

• • • • • • •

The next week, Mr. Cheung was gone. He'd taught Mom and Dad as much as he could. Now they were on their own.

That morning, Dad stood in the kitchen, giddy with anticipation and nerves. The first few orders had gone by smoothly enough. Mostly coffee, toast and a couple of ham-and-egg sandwiches.

Then Mom walked up to the window to call an order. "Fried egg sandwich," she said.

He asked her to repeat herself.

"Fried egg sandwich," she said again.

Dad nodded, straight-faced. He picked up the menu, scrolling down the pages until he saw it: "Fried egg sandwich." There was no description. Mr. Cheung had never mentioned a fried egg sandwich. He definitely hadn't gotten around to teaching it.

So Dad walked over to the griddle. He pulled out two slices of bread, buttered one side of each and placed them down on the hot surface. Then he took an egg out of the refrigerator and cracked it over the griddle. It hissed and sizzled, the edges quickly crisping and hardening into a lace skirt.

With the easy part done, he had to take a moment to think.

Fried egg sandwich.

Surely there was more to it? Who would pay for two slices of bread and an egg?

So he ran through all of the other sandwiches on his menu. The most popular sandwiches, the ones that Mr. Cheung had taught him, all had another thing in common. They all had lettuce. The BLT, turkey, and chicken salad sandwiches all had a piece of crisp iceberg lettuce inside. Mr. Cheung had told him that texture was important in Western cooking—that lettuce could add that extra bit of crunch.

So Dad walked over to the refrigerator and grabbed a head of lettuce. He scrunched his brow, then laid two lettuce leaves atop the fried egg before covering it with the second piece of bread.

Mom took the plate out and Dad followed her into the dining room. He pretended he was checking on something behind the counter. He watched as the man picked up his sandwich. But just as he was about to take a bite, something stopped him and he put the sandwich back down on the plate.

The man lifted up the top piece of bread. A puzzled expression spread over his face. He picked off the lettuce with his fingers, tossing it aside on the plate. Then he closed up the sandwich and took a big bite. Within minutes, he'd eaten the whole thing.

Dad quickly disappeared back into the kitchen.

"Fried egg sandwich," he repeated to himself. "Toast. Fried egg. No lettuce."

He was learning.

TOP LEFT: Don Mee Seafood Restaurant is a Victoria, BC, institution. TOP RIGHT: Peter Li (seated in booth) is the owner of Diana Restaurant in Drumheller, AB. ABOVE: The *Star Trek* mural is just one of the Trekkie tourist attractions in Vulcan, AB.

LEFT: Bing's #1 Restaurant in Stony Plain, AB, is a popular local meeting place that's been run by three generations of the Choy family. BELOW: The dining room at Bing's is full of customers. William Choy, in the background, works in the restaurant's kitchen between appointments for his second job—mayor of Stony Plain. FACING PAGE, TOP: Lan Huynh is the owner of Thai Woks N'go in Glendon, AB, a restaurant that sells "Chinese pierogis." FACING PAGE, BOTTOM: Thai Woks N'go is located at a prime spot in Glendon, across the street from the world's largest perogy.

FACING PAGE, TOP: Moon's Cafe in Grenfell, SK, is run by Moon Wei. FACING PAGE, BOTTOM: Su Fen Li runs Choy's Restaurant in Boissevain, MB, with her husband. Li moved from Guangdong to Canada ten years ago with her husband. TOP: Overlooking the buffet table at Ling Lee's Chinese Cuisine, a Chinese restaurant inside a curling club in Thunder Bay, ON, is a giant curling-themed mural. ABOVE: The buffet table at Ling Lee's features many of the classic chop suey dishes, plus "Bon Bon ribs," a Thunder Bay specialty.

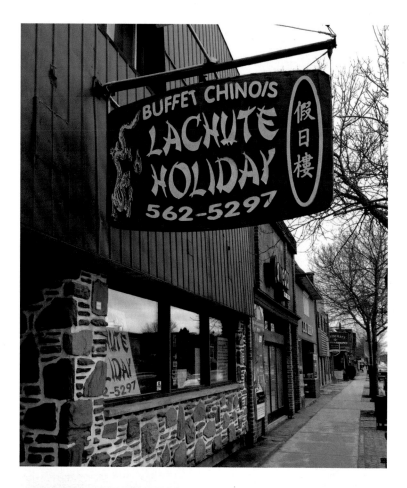

ABOVE: Lachute Holiday is a Chinese restaurant run by Guang Xiu Zhang and located in Lachute, QC. LEFT: "Fried macaroni" is a regional Chinese-Canadian specialty in Quebec. FACING PAGE: Restaurant Wong in Quebec City, QC, was built by Fred Wong, who left China in 1922. His grandson, Steven Wong, now runs the restaurant.

ABOVE: The Chow Family restaurant in Truro, NS, has a distinctive exterior. RIGHT: *Maneki-neko*, or "fortune cat," is a good-luck symbol commonly found in many Chinese restaurants. FACING PAGE, TOP: Richard Yu is the owner of Canton Restaurant in Deer Lake, NS. FACING PAGE, BOTTOM: Our tiny white rental car looked only slightly the worse for wear after two weeks on the road.

ABOVE: The Kwang Tung Restaurant is the only Chinese restaurant on tiny Fogo Island, NL. FAR LEFT: Since the ferry was shut down due to stormy conditions, this tiny twenty-seat plane brought us to Fogo Island. LEFT: The Kwang Tung is run by Feng Zhu Huang, who operates the restaurant on her own 365 days a year.

RIGHT: Ye Ye (left) and Ah Ngeen (right), pose for their "official" Canadian wedding photo. *Photo courtesy of Jennie Jung*
BELOW: Dad (centre) poses with his friends in Guangzhou. *Photo courtesy of the Hui family*
FACING PAGE: This professional photo of Dad was taken in Guangzhou before he came to Canada. *Photo courtesy of the Hui family*

ABOVE: Mom and Dad were married in St. Francis Xavier church, then located in Vancouver's Chinatown. *Photo courtesy of the Hui family*

FACING PAGE, TOP: This photo of the family was taken on Mom and Dad's wedding day in Vancouver's Chinatown. From left to right, back row: Dad, Mom, Ah Ngeen and Ye Ye. Front row: Aunt Janice and Aunt Jennie. *Photo courtesy of the Hui family.*

FACING PAGE, BOTTOM: Mom poses inside the Legion Cafe dining room. *Photo courtesy of the Hui family*

LEFT: Dad works in the Legion Cafe kitchen while Mom stands in the background, holding Pansy. *Photo courtesy of the Hui family* BELOW: This photograph shows the misspelled "Canadian and Chinise Cuisine" sign at the Legion Cafe, with Mom, Dad and a friend standing in front of the restaurant. *Photo courtesy of the Hui family*

Deer Lake, NL.

Spring 2016

W E DROVE OFF the ship, past a small cluster of homes painted blue, red and yellow. From the Trans-Canada Highway, we took in the snow-covered rock that seemed to stretch on forever. It felt like we were the only ones on the island. There was only our car and the highway.

About three hours into our drive, we stopped in a town called Deer Lake, about thirty minutes past Corner Brook. It was time for lunch. Just off the highway, sandwiched between an A&W and a Subway, was a white trailer-style building. The word "CANTON" was painted in big block letters in red on the side of the building. Next to it, the Chinese simplified characters for "Guangdong."

Anthony needed another break from Chinese. There was a pizza place down the road, he said. He'd wait for me there. As I pulled open the door, a handmade sign caught my eye. "Chow mein on our menu is cabbage," it read.

Inside the Canton Restaurant, a middle-aged man

greeted me from behind the counter. He looked about fifty. Despite the stained apron around his waist, he had a professorial look to him. His hair was neatly trimmed, and he wore a smart-looking zip-up vest over his plaid shirt. He introduced himself in Cantonese as Richard Yu, the owner of the restaurant.

The way he spoke, as if he gave thought to every word, reminded me of Dad. He looked a lot like him too, with a thin face and high cheekbones. Every once in a while, he smiled, causing the corners of his eyes to crinkle. He was right in the middle of the lunch rush, he said apologetically. But if I didn't mind waiting, he could come talk to me once things died down.

So I sat at a table near the front of the room, watching as he hurried back and forth between the kitchen and the dining room. The dining room itself was huge, split into two levels, with about thirty tables. The walls were white with green wainscotting. The door frames and trims were painted red. In the middle of the room was one long table with over a dozen people seated around it, mostly seniors having their lunch. A handful of other families and couples were there too. And every few minutes, the door would open and in would walk another guy in a flannel shirt and work boots, ordering take out for lunch.

I studied the menu, a mostly familiar collection of classic chop suey dishes (egg rolls, chicken guy ding, sweet and sour pork), along with "Canadian" ones (fish and chips, liver dinner and T-bone steak). The wings were on special, either deep-fried in batter or drenched in honey-garlic sauce.

About ten minutes later, Mr. Yu came over to sit down. Like my dad, he was from Toisan and had moved to Vancouver in his twenties. Like my dad, he had daughters.

He'd been a high school science teacher in China, something my dad only aspired to. But when he arrived in Vancouver, he didn't have the luxury of going back to school to get the credentials he needed to continue teaching. He needed to earn money right away to support his family. So he went into the restaurant business.

It was the Goldilocks approach that had led them to Deer Lake, he said. They liked Vancouver, with all of the amenities for Chinese immigrants. But there were already so many Chinese restaurants there. Competition was stiff, so they had to work all the time. Plus the living costs were high. What did it matter that there was a Chinese New Year parade when they didn't have time to go see it?

They heard through acquaintances that Newfoundland was a nice place to live. So the family moved to Corner Brook, where Mr. Yu took over a Chinese restaurant. But that city wasn't right either. The restaurant was too quiet. It had a bad reputation among locals because of previous owners, they learned. And there was no parking—essential, given the Newfoundland winter weather.

So they moved again, this time to Deer Lake. Finally, Mr. Yu said, they felt like they were home. The town, with just under five thousand residents, felt peaceful. The people were nice. And here, competition wasn't an issue. Canton was, at least at the beginning, the only Chinese restaurant in town.

"We made the right decision," he said. "I'm satisfied with my life right now. My kids have grown up, my business is steady, and I have peace of mind."

He'd had to make adjustments for the region, he said. Some of the recipes didn't translate in Newfoundland. Ribs, for example. In Vancouver, he'd had his recipe for spareribs perfected. He'd deep fry them before coating them in a sauce—sweet and sour or honey garlic—so that they were crispy on the outside but tender on the inside. They'd always been a hit in Vancouver.

But when he made the same ribs for his Newfoundland customers, they were unimpressed. "They said, 'Even a dog wouldn't eat this!'" Mr. Yu said, chuckling. It took him a while to figure out the key difference. His new customers in Newfoundland were much, much older than the ones he'd had in BC. The crunchy ribs were hard on their teeth. Or at least, on the teeth they had left. Newfoundland has the oldest median age in the entire country. Over 20 per cent of the population in Deer Lake is over the age of sixty-five.

So he started braising his ribs, cooking them slowly under low heat until they were soft and tender, falling off the bone. They were an immediate hit.

We'd already seen a number of these regional variations along our trip. There was ginger beef back in the Prairies. In Quebec, we'd found "fried macaroni," stir-fried pasta with soy sauce, meat and veggies. In my research, I'd also come across "Peterborough won-tons" (deep-fried wonton skins, without the meat fillings), and the Timmins, ON, custom of serving all Chinese dishes with a side of toast. And here in Newfoundland, it was braised ribs.

"When you fail, you learn," Mr. Yu said. "You learn from your mistakes."

· · · · · · ·

The restaurant was beginning to fill up again, which I took as my cue to get out of the way. But first, I asked about the sign at the door.

"What does that mean, that your chow mein is made with cabbage?'"

"Another Newfoundland thing," he said.

The first Chinese restaurateurs had to improvise because they weren't able to find Chinese ingredients, he said. But the problem was especially pronounced in Newfoundland. It was nearly impossible to get even basic ingredients, like soy sauce or bok choy, imported onto the island. Even egg noodles—the "mein" in "chow mein"—were difficult to come by. One of those enterprising early restaurateurs improvised by cutting cabbage into thin strips, so that they'd resemble, at least in appearance, thin noodles. He started calling it chow mein, and it stuck.

To this day, "chow mein" in Newfoundland means thin strips of cabbage, stir-fried with veggies and meat. For noodles, Mr. Yu said, you have to ask for them specifically, by ordering "Cantonese chow mein on noodles." The sign on the door was a recent addition, he said, after tourists started getting confused.

I decided to order my own container of Newfoundland chow mein, to go. As I walked out with the Styrofoam bowl, Mr. Yu waved goodbye. He nodded at the bag in my hands.

"You won't find anything like this in Vancouver," he said, a mischievous glint in his eye.

Back in the car, I found Anthony sitting with a pizza box in his lap.

"I got this for you," he said, handing me a small personal-sized pizza box. I opened the lid to find a pizza covered with a white sauce. Studded across the top were pieces of pink shrimp, small scallops and what looked like chunks of lobster meat, all of it under a blanket of cheese. "Apparently it's a Newfoundland thing," he said.

I grabbed a slice, then took a bite. The seafood tasted like it was from frozen, and all of it was overcooked—the textures of the shellfish indistinguishable from the rubbery mushrooms. The cheese tasted like salt and little else. I winced and handed the box back to Anthony.

Then I pried the lid off the Styrofoam container from Canton. Sure enough, inside were thin strips of cabbage, stir-fried with plump pieces of chicken, carrots and onions. Using a plastic fork, I took a big bite. It tasted familiar—the sweetness of the veggies, the juicy chicken and a hint of soy and sesame, like chow mein without the crunchy noodles. What it lacked in texture it made up for with a richness in flavor. The cabbage added a depth to the dish. It was even more savoury, even more umami than a traditional chow mein.

"What is that?" Anthony said, leaning over and looking into my bowl.

"Chow mein," I said happily. "It's a Newfoundland thing."

And it was. This dish, from its origin story, to its ingredients, to its execution—it was utterly and completely Newfoundland.

It told the story of this place. It was as Canadian as it was Chinese.

"When you fail, you learn," Mr. Yu had said. "The point is that you keep going."

Just weeks earlier, I had been so dismissive of this food as "fake Chinese." Now I realized I had been completely wrong. This ad-hoc cuisine, and the families behind it, were quintessentially Chinese. It was pure entrepreneurialism. Out of cabbage, they'd made noodles. Out of a bucket and water, they'd grown bean sprouts. They had created a cuisine that was a testament to creativity, perseverance and resourcefulness. This chop suey cuisine wasn't fake Chinese—but instead, the most Chinese of all.

. . . .

In late afternoon, Anthony and I arrived in Gander, where we would stay the night.

The small city is home to over eleven thousand—big enough for its own shopping mall, with a couple dozen stores, and a local CBC station. It's also the city that gained international attention after welcoming thousands of stranded passengers after the 9/11 attacks forced the landing of several airliners. (The city's outpouring of generosity toward these complete strangers would later became the subject of the Broadway musical *Come from Away*.)

After a quick dinner at the Country Kitchen inside the mall (fish and chips for me, poutine for Anthony), we returned to our hotel with plans to depart early the next morning for Fogo Island.

All those months earlier as I was plotting out our trip, my editors and I had briefly talked about ending the trip in Ontario instead of driving all the way to the East Coast. It would have been significantly cheaper to stop in Toronto. But there was the one restaurant I really wanted to visit, all the way out on Fogo Island. After stumbling across the blog post about the Fogo restaurant, I had found a photo of the woman who ran the Chinese restaurant on Fogo Island. The photo haunted me. Like many, I had only learned about Fogo Island recently, after the opening of a splashy hotel built there by tech millionaire (and Newfoundlander) Zita Cobb. The hotel and the celebrities it attracts—everyone from Justin Trudeau to Gwyneth Paltrow—had suddenly shone a giant spotlight on the tiny island. But outside of the fancy hotel, what little I knew of the island was that it was tiny, secluded and about as remote as it gets. I couldn't shake the idea of this woman running a Chinese restaurant there, alone. I knew I had to meet her. My editors agreed that the extra mileage would be worth it. And so, much of the trip was designed around my hopes of eventually getting to Fogo Island.

We had planned to take the ferry to Fogo the next morning. It was a small government-run vessel that would have taken about an hour and fifteen minutes to transport us along with our car to the island. But as I checked the ferry's website that night in our hotel room to confirm the departure time, I saw that the storm that had dogged us back in Cape Breton wasn't done with us yet. Our ferry had been cancelled. Instead, the province had chartered an Air Labrador flight to hop back and forth between Gander and Fogo, and it was our only alternative to get to the island. The cost was the same as the ferry, and the flight would take just half an hour—one-third the amount of time as the ferry. The only catch? We wouldn't be able to bring our car with us.

I did a quick search for taxi services on Fogo, glanced at a few search results that popped up and went to bed.

• • • • • • •

The next morning, we woke up early, with plans of catching the first flight out from Gander airport. Walking into the terminal was like travelling back in time. It had originally opened in 1938, and at the time, with its four paved runways, was the world's largest airport. As the only airport in the Maritimes, it was strategically located for bomber aircrafts that required refuelling and maintenance before continuing overseas. Until the 1950s, it remained one of the busiest airports in the world.

But in the 1960s, the invention of jet aircrafts that didn't need refuelling ended all that. And the airport, a temple of Modernist architecture, looked like it hadn't been touched since. The international lounge was like a set from *Mad Men*, with Mondrian tile patterned floors, orange walls and mid-century modern furniture.

Many of the airline counters were still setting up and the Air Labrador counter wasn't yet open. Sitting next to the counter was a man who looked to be in his forties who wore a camouflage jacket with a deer emblazoned on the back and a camouflage cap. He was surrounded by large boxes and duffle bags.

"This the flight to Fogo?" I asked.

He nodded and introduced himself as Cecil. He was just returning to Fogo after several months of working near Toronto. The fisheries on Fogo aren't what they used to be. So he (and many Fogo locals) go off-island at least part of each year for work.

"This your first time on Fogo?" he asked.

I said that it was, and that we were planning on doing some sightseeing on the island.

"Who's gonna take you around?" he asked.

I told him we hoped to rent a taxi or a car once we arrived.

He scrunched his eyebrows and cocked his chin. "Taxi?" he asked. He seemed skeptical.

I said that I'd seen them online. Fogo Island had become such a hot spot for tourists recently, surely it wouldn't be hard to get a taxi.

He nodded his head slowly but seemed unconvinced. A few minutes later, he added, "Tell you what, if you get stuck, just give me a call. I'll take you around."

I just smiled. It was a nice offer, considering we'd only just met. But I told him we'd be okay.

Not long after, a man with a clipboard wandered over to us to check us in. It was just the three of us for the flight, he said. Once we were ready, he'd take us out to the aircraft.

So Cecil, Anthony and I followed the man through a sliding glass door and directly onto the snow-covered tarmac. There, a Twin Otter aircraft was waiting for us. As Cecil passed his bags to the handlers, Anthony and I climbed the steps up into the cabin. It was the smallest plane I'd ever been in, about twenty seats in total. It was probably the oldest plane I'd been in too, nothing like the sleek airbuses and Dreamliners I'd grown accustomed to as a flight attendant. The cabin looked as if it hadn't been updated since the 1960s, and had the feel of a school bus, with blue bench-style seating and walls painted turquoise and white.

"Where should we sit?" I asked Anthony.

He looked around the empty cabin.

"Anywhere we want, I guess."

As we settled in our seats, I realized that where there would normally be a door separating the flight deck from the cabin was instead an open space. I thought back to the security training I'd had working as a flight attendant. It had been just a few years after 9/11, and the importance of preventing anyone from entering the flight deck had been drilled into us. But today, the pilot and his first officer were just a few arm's lengths away. We watched as they conducted their pre-flight inspections, checking dials, flipping through manuals, speaking with each other in hushed tones.

A few minutes later, we were ready to go. With a few more flips of some switches, we were taxiing toward the runway. We could feel each and every bump on the pavement. We began gaining speed, hurtling forward with the cabin shaking and jolting the entire time. Finally, with a last gasp of effort, the plane lifted off into the air. Below us was Newfoundland—all tree and rock and snow-covered lakes. Anthony and I fell into silence, both of us gazing out the window. From above, the Atlantic Ocean looked ready to swallow the island whole.

Just twenty minutes later, it was time for descent. I scanned the landscape below us, looking for signs of civilization. But the island looked untouched. The plane touched down on the runway, next to a single, temporary-looking building that looked to be in the middle of nowhere.

We walked out onto the tarmac and into the airport. All the while, I looked for some kind of transportation—a rental car kiosk, a taxi stand or at least a bus kiosk. But there was only a tiny parking lot next to the terminal with a couple of cars parked. Otherwise, there was nothing but empty fields and forest.

Inside the one-room terminal, there was only a single employee working behind a counter, selling plane tickets. I noticed a bulletin board on the wall. Pinned to it was a business card advertising a taxi service. It looked to be the same one I had seen online the day before. I passed the card to Anthony and asked him to call it. Meanwhile, I stood in line, waiting to speak with the airport employee.

A few moments later, Anthony appeared by my side. "He said the taxi service hasn't been in business since 2013."

"What?"

"There's no taxi service," he repeated.

I searched on my phone for "Fogo Island" and "taxi," but sure enough, the number that popped up was the same as the one on the business card.

The airport was at least ten kilometres from town. And in this weather, walking was not an option.

Now what?

I turned around to look for Cecil, but he was nowhere to be found. Behind me in line was a young man who looked like he might be a local.

"Excuse me," I said. He looked up. I explained to him what had happened, how we'd found ourselves stranded.

"I don't suppose you might know someone we can hire for the day to drive us around?"

He thought about it for a few moments. Then he turned to the group of men standing behind him.

"Hey guys, do you know anyone who can drive them around?"

I could see them thinking about it, mumbling to each other, conferring. I looked at Anthony, who looked at the men, who looked back at us.

A few moments later, from across the room, a man's voice piped up. "They can take my car."

I whipped my head around to see where the voice was coming from. It was an older man with white hair. He was walking toward us, one of his arms outstretched with a set of keys.

I was stunned. I turned to look at Anthony, who looked similarly taken aback.

I tried to speak. "I—we—what?"

I couldn't tell if he was joking. He was a complete stranger. *We* were complete strangers.

A few feet away, the woman he was with nodded in encouragement. They were completely serious.

"We're heading to Gander for the day so we don't need it," he said. Gander—the city famous for its generosity to strangers. "Just leave the keys at the counter when you're done."

I looked at Anthony, who still looked stunned. I couldn't imagine such a thing happening back home.

The guys standing around the airport were all nodding their heads in agreement. They seemed to think this was normal—as if this type of generosity, and trust, was typical. From their reactions, I suspected, perhaps it was—at least here in Newfoundland.

I asked him his name, and he introduced himself as Lloyd Bailey.

"Lloyd, you have no idea how grateful we are."

He just shrugged. "It's nothing, really," he said.

Before he and his wife walked away, I called out one last time. "Lloyd, are you sure? You're not worried we'll steal your car and you'll never see it again?"

He just laughed. He gestured around him at the empty fields and ocean surrounding us. "It's an island," he said. "You'd have nowhere to take it."

A few minutes later, Anthony turned the keys in the ignition of Lloyd's Hyundai sedan. The dashboard lit up and the engine roared to life. We were on our way.

Abbotsford, BC.

1977–84

OST MORNINGS, MY parents were at the Legion by eight. Mom would flip the "Closed" sign to "Open" and greet the occasional customer already standing outside waiting for their morning coffee.

She'd get the coffee started right away, then count the cash at the register, making sure the totals she'd added up the night before were still correct. Dad would head straight into the kitchen. There wasn't much to do to prepare breakfast. Most mornings, they'd have fewer than ten breakfast customers, and most would just order coffee. Maybe toast—a bowl of cereal at most.

Instead, while the dining room slowly filled up, Dad would begin getting lunch ready.

As instructed by Mr. Cheung, he'd decide what soup to put on special based on what was left over from the night before. If there was extra chicken, he'd make chicken noodle soup or cream of chicken. If it was carrots and peas, he'd make a vegetable medley. He would spell the soup out in white letters on a black magnet board, under the words "Today's Special." Next he'd figure out the sandwich special—hot beef, or hot turkey, or maybe a clubhouse. By about ten most mornings, the restaurant would quiet down again. Dad would wash the dishes, rinsing out coffee mugs and toast crumbs.

And soon, it was time for lunch. This was normally their busiest time. Construction workers from the job site across the street, workers from nearby offices and some of the elderly locals who had become regulars over the years would all stream in. On an average day, they would see about fifty customers.

On especially busy days, when the customers all seemed to walk in at the same time, Mom would scribble out the orders frantically. "H + E" —ham and egg—she'd scrawl on her pad, slamming it down on the counter for Dad. "B + E"—bacon and eggs. She felt like she was everywhere at once—greeting people as they walked in, taking orders, dropping off dishes and calculating bills at the end of the meal.

And Dad was running around inside the kitchen. Slicing sandwiches. Sloshing hot soup into bowls. Flipping toast on the griddle. Whenever it felt like it was too much, he would calmly talk to himself, walking through the checklist of things to be done.

Toast bread. Warm beef. Slice tomato. Cheese.

The customers arrived, they ordered, they ate and they left. This would happen over and over and over again, until about two in the afternoon.

And suddenly it would be quiet again. Mom would sweep

or finish taking care of the books. She hated when she was in the middle of a long calculation, her head a jumble of numbers, and a new customer would walk in. She'd greet them, take their order, then have to start again from the beginning. Other afternoons, people would just come in to say hello— the regulars who got to know Mom by name and would sit for hours just to chat.

Dinner was normally slow at the Legion, even slower than breakfast.

Very rarely did people go out for dinner or leave their houses at all in the evenings in Abbotsford. Many of them were farmers who were up at dawn and in bed by eight. Most had barely a few dollars to scratch together.

So Mom and Dad would eat their own dinner. They'd have whatever was in the restaurant that day. If there was a giant roast turkey in the fridge, Dad would set aside the drumstick— the best part—early in the day so Mom could have it with dinner. He'd steam some bok choy or sui choy he'd buy on the weekends in Vancouver. All of it they'd eat with steamed rice Dad made in a rice cooker in the kitchen.

Once in a while, a customer would walk in while they were having their dinner. "They'd see the food on our plates— steamed vegetables and rice—and they felt badly for us," Mom said. They didn't understand that these simple dishes, to Mom and Dad, were the most comforting, and reminded them most of home.

Every Sunday was a day off. Abbotsford was still heavily religious, and the entire town was shut down on Sundays. So on those days, Mom and Dad would drive their little yellow

Chevette around (Dad bought the car from a regular, who owned the used car lot down the street). Some weekends, they would drive the hour west to Vancouver to see Po Po, Uncle Zachary and his kids. Or occasionally, they would see Ye Ye, Ah Ngeen and my aunts. Ye Ye had cooled down, at least enough to let them in for stiff visits.

Other times, they would head south of the border, driving into Bellingham. The groceries in Bellingham were cheaper and they could stock up with what they needed for the restaurant there. Then they would treat themselves to the brunch buffet at their favourite restaurant in Bellingham, gorging on crab legs and oysters and everything else on offer.

• • • • • • • •

The few orders that did come in at night usually came from the bar across the hall. The bar didn't have its own kitchen, so occasionally the Legion members, some of them older men who would sit and drink at the bar for hours, would order something to eat to soak up all that liquor. Others had a daily routine, where they would spend a few hours in the restaurant to break up an otherwise full day of drinking.

Some customers would come in already drunk at nine in the morning, nursing the same cup of coffee until lunch. Others would come in just as Mom and Dad were about to close around nine or ten at night. They'd want to chat, and then sit and want to talk for hours. Dad would silently fume from the kitchen, but Mom never kicked them out. Often these same customers would return a few days later, and maybe order French fries. And then a full meal. And again, and again, until they became regulars.

Occasionally, the drunk customers would get nasty. Even the seemingly pleasant ones they would otherwise make small talk with in the hallways and on the streets. After a few drinks, they would turn. "You're a chink!" they would shout at my mom or dad.

When things got especially bad, the staff from the bar across the hall would sometimes step in to help. And there was a police station down the road, which meant a lot of police officers became regulars. They would stop in throughout the day for coffee, and help out when they saw an especially unruly customer.

One night, a man Mom recognized as having been to the restaurant before walked in. But this night, he was stumbling and slurring. He stank of liquor. As Mom walked past him carrying two plates of food to a customer, he said he wanted to order food.

"Please sit down," she said to him. "I'll be with you in just a moment."

But the man grew irritated, belligerent. He shouted that he was hungry, and that she needed to serve him right away.

"Why won't you serve me?" he shouted, so loudly the entire dining room could hear. Loud enough that Dad heard him in the kitchen and came out to the dining room to see what was happening.

"If you won't serve me, why do you have a restaurant, you stupid chink?" he screamed. He pointed at the bump protruding from behind Mom's apron—she was visibly pregnant with my sister Pansy. "Don't have another kid, you stupid chink!"

Dad walked straight toward them, placing himself between Mom and the man.

"You need to leave," he said in the calmest voice he could manage.

The man just leered down at Dad, enraged. His face was red and his eyes were wild.

Panicked, Mom ran behind the counter and grabbed a large tray. She squeezed herself between the man and Dad, covering her pregnant belly with the tray. She began shouting. "I'm calling 911!" she screamed. "I'm calling 911!"

She kept shouting like this for a few minutes until the man eventually just slumped over. It wasn't clear whether he felt defeated or simply lost interest. Either way, he turned around and stumbled toward the door.

I sat there silently, feeling slightly sick as she recounted this. I had assumed they'd had to deal with stuff like this, but never actually heard details.

"How did you feel afterward?" I asked her.

She just shrugged. "Many of them only acted that way when they drank," she said. She didn't think those occasional incidents and behaviours meant the people themselves were racist— a distinction I found baffling. *Why did it matter whether we called them racist,* I thought, *if their actions were clearly racist?*

But Mom was more interested in explaining their behaviour. Many of them were immigrants themselves, Eastern Europeans who had fled to Canada with their own stories of survival. Even many of the white locals—those who had been born in Abbotsford and lived there their whole lives—were living at or just below the poverty line, she said. They all had their own challenges, and were wondering why their lives hadn't turned out the way they wanted. They were looking for someone to blame. Mom and Dad stood out. So this made them the target.

I wondered if she was being overly generous. Or maybe she was simply downplaying the matter. Maybe it was easier for her to explain away the behaviour. She shrugged again. "We had a lot in common, but they looked down on us," she said.

• • • • • • •

By their second year at the Legion, Mom and Dad had settled into a routine and started to make friends.

There was Carl, an older European man who had formerly run the Ukrainian restaurant up the street. His wife had died some years ago. He had spent all his time when he was younger working and didn't have many friends now that he was retired. The Legion became his regular hangout, and Mom and Dad his friends. Over cups of coffee, they would trade stories from their restaurants about the drunk customers who caused a commotion, or the ones who would come in each day and order nothing but coffee. They also traded recipes—Carl taught Dad how to make cabbage rolls and Dad showed him some of the dishes he had learned to make at the Nanking.

There was also a retired schoolteacher in her seventies who came in often. She and Mom would chat for hours over coffee. As Mom got closer to delivering Pansy, the woman helped prepare her. She taught Mom what she'd learned from teaching—about when the baby's brain development was most active, the best methods for teaching babies, and whether it would be a problem to speak both English and Chinese with a newborn.

One winter day, in the thick of her pregnancy, Mom watched as heavy sheets of snow fell outside the restaurant. The restaurant and streets were dead silent, and they were debating whether to shut down the restaurant for the day. Just as they were getting ready to close, Mom saw a car turn the corner and slow down to park in front of the restaurant. It was the retired teacher, walking gingerly toward the restaurant carrying a large platter in her hands.

"What are you doing here?" Mom asked.

The woman lifted the lid from the platter and steam rose up, carrying with it a vaguely perfumed scent. It was egg custard. My mom had been having pregnancy cravings the day before. She'd gone on and on to the woman about the milk custard she used to eat in Hong Kong. So the woman had made for Mom her own version of custard—a thicker European version. Mom almost wept, she was so grateful. She took a large spoonful. It was warm and sweet and delicious. It tasted like home.

• • • • • • •

On August 15, 1978, Pansy was born. Mom looked down at this squirming baby, her hair matted and wild, her face red from crying. The same way Po Po had looked at Mom. The way Ah Ngeen had looked at Dad.

The plan, at least at first, was to keep Pansy at the restaurant. Maternity leave wasn't even an idea that crossed their minds.

Dad couldn't run the cafe on his own and they couldn't afford to hire a waitress. So they cleared out some space in the storage room. They put her bassinet and diapers between the canned vegetables and boxes of coffee filters.

All day long, Mom would run back and forth. In the dining room, she'd wait tables and serve customers just as she had before. Only now she'd have to run into the storage room every few minutes to check on Pansy as she slept. Mom would run herself dizzy going back and forth between customers and the screaming infant. Every feeding or diaper change would set things back in the restaurant. She was exhausted.

As Pansy grew older, she became more curious by the day. She grew out of her bassinet, so they set up a small bed in the storage room instead. This they put behind a baby gate, to prevent her from running out into the dining room or kitchen during service.

One day, Mom left her like that in the storage room. She was only gone for a few minutes to check on customers. But when she returned, she saw that Pansy had grabbed hold of something, and was spreading it everywhere, including on herself. All over her hands and face was a white powder, smeared in giant circles.

Mom scanned the room, frantically trying to figure out what it was. She called Dad over from the kitchen to help. The bag of flour was intact and untouched, still sitting on the shelf. So were the baking soda and the cornstarch.

Eventually, her eyes fell on a mouse trap that had been set up in the corner of the room. She pointed it out to Dad, and he walked over to pick it up. He flipped it over, emptying the contents. Into his hands fell a white powder that looked just like the stuff on Pansy's face.

Rodenticide.

They raced to the hospital.

At the hospital, they relayed to the nurses what had happened. Their stone-faced reactions said it all: *Are you kidding me?*

And then Mom and Dad sat there in anguish. They thought about what they could have done differently. They couldn't believe how careless they'd been.

Eventually, the doctor came out to say Pansy was fine. It didn't look like she had swallowed or ingested the powder. She had just been playing with it, smearing it on her cheeks like makeup.

He put Pansy, still squirming and laughing, into my mom's arms. Then they went home.

They made the decision to hire a babysitter the next day.

• • • • • • •

After a few years in Abbotsford, some of the locals grew used to seeing Mom and Dad around, walking up the street pushing Pansy in her stroller. But others still treated them like a curiosity.

There were only a couple of other Chinese families in town that Mom and Dad knew of. There was the family who ran the restaurant at the Park Inn, the "fancy" Chinese place. They met briefly, the other family popping in to say hello as soon as my parents took over the Legion. But as soon as they heard that Mom and Dad didn't play mah-jong, they quickly lost interest. My parents never heard from them again.

And there was one other Chinese man who moved in briefly, not long after my parents. He opened a Chinese restaurant across from Sevenoaks mall called Victory. But not long after, he was at the Legion, complaining to Dad about how there were no customers in Abbotsford. Soon, he was leaving the lights off in the restaurant to avoid paying the electricity. Then he packed up and left Abbotsford altogether.

But around 1980, a curious thing happened. Around that time, news surrounding the Vietnam War was changing. The stories were now focusing on the devastation the war had caused, and the many homes and lives it had destroyed. Hundreds of thousands of Vietnamese were fleeing their country in boats, while groups like the UN, and countries like Canada, came to their aid.

Tens of thousands of these "Vietnamese boat people" wound up in Canada as refugees. And because of Abbotsford's large religious community, about two hundred of these families wound up there, many of them sponsored by local churches.

Almost overnight, there were hundreds of other East Asians in Abbotsford. Sure, they were from an entirely different country with a different culture and history. But they looked a little like my parents—at least to the locals in Abbotsford. Like Mom and Dad, they too were outsiders.

Suddenly my parents found that they stuck out just a little bit less.

At first, Mom and Dad greeted this with amused detachment. They felt sympathy for these newcomers, but were so busy just trying to run their restaurant and keep afloat themselves. Mom was also pregnant with a second child, Amber. So they gave them little thought.

But one day, a Vietnamese man walked into the Legion. He was the first of the refugees to come into the restaurant. Many of them had taken jobs on the farms and didn't have money to be eating at restaurants. But that day, the man approached Mom timidly, greeting her with a smile and introducing himself.

He explained that his family was staying with a white family from the church. They were kind and generous, he said. They had treated his family warmly and given them a place to live and food to eat. But day after day, the meals the family fed them were so completely foreign. He wanted nothing more than a bowl of steamed white rice. He glanced up at her nervously.

Mom went into the kitchen to tell Dad, who scooped a generous mound of plump white rice into a bowl. The both of them returned to the dining room, then watched as the man gulped down the contents in big, greedy bites. Afterward, he thanked them over and over again.

Mom shook her head. "Anytime," she said. "Come back with your family anytime."

From that point on, the man would return periodically with his wife and kids in tow. Each time, Mom and Dad would serve them rice with steamed Chinese vegetables, or broth made out of pork bones, or whatever else they were able to scrape together. The dishes were mostly Chinese, not Vietnamese. But there were commonalities. Vietnam had, after all, once been a Chinese colony. Rice and noodles. The wok. Stir-fries. Soy sauce.

Gradually, some of the man's friends began to frequent the cafe as well. As they got to know each other, Mom would try to give them stuff, trying to pass on some of their old household items, like Pansy's old baby clothes or other things they no longer needed around the house. But they always refused. The clothes, the household items—all of that stuff they were already getting from their sponsor families. The food was what they wanted. It was the food that comforted them.

They also began turning to Mom and Dad for advice. A few of the Vietnamese men moved into construction, doing repairs on houses and buildings in the area. They asked Dad about starting a business—how to find the right forms to fill out, how to do their basic accounting. "Ah Hong Goh," or "Big brother John," they would call him.

It seemed like such a short time ago that Mom and Dad had been the newcomers. They had been the ones fumbling around trying to figure out how to start their lives in a new place. Friends and strangers had stepped in to help them and to provide advice. And now they were the ones giving advice.

It hadn't always been easy, but this country and this community had been good to them, allowing them to move in and start their new lives. Mom and Dad felt grateful for this. Now, they were grateful for the chance to pass this on. It made them feel good.

• • • • • • •

In 1981, the company that ran the Park Inn, the "fancy" Chinese restaurant in Abbotsford, called my parents. They wanted to know if Mom and Dad would want to take over. They walked over to take a look. They'd walked past the hotel many times in the past. It was just a five-minute walk from the Legion, and they'd gawked enviously at the lobby and huge dining room.

But that day they walked inside, into the dining room. They took in the mahogany wood tables, oak chairs with uphol-stered cushions. Compared with the Legion, with its vinyl chairs and the counter Dad had built out of plywood, the Park Inn looked like a five-star restaurant. It was without a doubt the fanciest place in Abbotsford.

They decided to sign on, on a trial basis. Mom and Dad would come on board as employees before deciding whether or not to take over altogether.

From the first day, they were shocked at how different things were at the Park. There were easily three times as many customers passing through each day. But here, they had staff—cooks to help Dad out in the kitchen, and waitresses out in the dining room to help Mom with the orders. And the Park was only open for breakfast and lunch. Suddenly, they went from working twelve hours each day to eight or nine. By this time, Mom and Dad had two kids, so this meant they had time to actually spend with my sisters each night.

After a few months, they agreed to take over the restaurant completely.

At first, Dad took the same approach as at the Legion. He kept things the same as they'd always been, using the same recipes and methods as the former owners. But they had seen by then in Vancouver that the most fashionable Chinese restaurants had buffets or "smorgasbords." The all-you-can-eat style of dining, popularized in Quebec in the 1960s by Chinese restaurateur Bill Wong, had spread all over Canada. For many customers who walked into the Park, it was what they expected from a Chinese restaurant.

So Dad decided to do a buffet. The restaurant already had warming tables and other equipment from its catering business. And it made his job easier. Instead of cooking every order individually, he and his cooks could prepare all of the dishes at once and only replenish throughout the day as necessary. It also limited the number of menu items he had to have available to customers, cutting down the number of ingredients he had to order and have on hand. The customers liked it too.

Taking over the Park meant a bigger income. Mom and Dad were keen savers, and just two years after starting the Legion, they'd bought their first home, a brand-new split-level on Astoria Crescent. With the money they were making at the Park, they were even able to buy a second home, an investment property they rented out on Geneva Court near the hospital. For the first time in either of their lives, they were comfortable. They were earning steady incomes and could afford small luxuries they'd never before imagined.

Every once in a while, Dad would look over at the buffet tables and think of Jingweicun. He'd remember eating boiled yams day after day. He would think back to those days on the farm, of how sparingly he'd had to portion his classmates' pork. *If there's food, you should eat it,* his relatives had told him before he left.

Now in front of him—entire platters covered with meat. Platters filled with flavours and textures and colours he'd never known existed. On slow days, they'd wind up giving away the unused food to hotel staff. The rest they would throw out in the garbage.

. . . .

One night in late July of 1983, Mom and Dad were just getting home from work when Mom began to feel a familiar aching in her stomach. By then, she was nine months pregnant with me, and recognized the pain right away as contractions. They jumped into the car, heading toward the hospital. Mom was admitted right away and prepped by the nurses for labour.

While they waited, Dad turned to Mom. "What do we do now?" he asked.

Pansy and Amber, then just four and two, were still at home with the babysitter, whose shift was long over. She had agreed to stay at the house while they dashed off to the hospital, but someone needed to go back to the house to relieve her. Dad suggested calling Po Po. But by then it was past midnight. Mom didn't want to wake her. Besides, Po Po didn't drive, meaning Uncle Zachary would have to drive her all the way from Vancouver. Mom didn't want to disturb them both. They didn't know what else to do. So Dad went home to take care of the girls. Mom stayed at the hospital, alone.

That night, she lay in her hospital bed, feeling scared and small. The contractions tore through her, causing her to convulse and scream out in pain, and there was no one to console her but the nurses. She had never before felt so alone.

I was born the next morning.

• • • • • • •

In 1984, the year I turned one, Mom and Dad decided to close the Park Inn restaurant for good.

That night at the hospital had left a lasting impression on them. They'd had enough of the isolation of living in Abbotsford. With three kids to care for, Mom yearned to be closer to Po Po and to Uncle Zachary and his three kids.

They handed the keys back to the Park Inn's owner. Dad got a job as head chef at a fancy buffet restaurant in Vancouver. And they put a down payment on a seventy-thousand-dollar house in East Vancouver.

As they packed up the Chevette to leave Abbotsford for the last time, they turned and tried to remember how strange and scary this place had initially seemed.

The little restaurant they'd built together had grown and grown.

Now, all they wanted to think about was where they were going. They talked excitedly about their new lives in Vancouver. Where they would go, and what they would eat first. It was time to move on.

Fogo Island, NL.

Spring 2016

W E SETTLED INTO Lloyd's purple Hyundai, Anthony adjusting quickly to the driver's seat. Just as he had with the little Fiat, he seemed to know by instinct where all the controls and levers would be placed. He paused before moving his foot onto the gas pedal, glancing over with a grin.

The entire island is about twenty-five kilometres long. Much of it is uninhabited, kilometre after kilometre of untouched boreal forest, weathered granite and roaring coastlines. Every direction we looked was another sweeping view, another epic landscape. I kept tugging on Anthony's sleeve to pull over.

"Look," I said, pointing at the waves crashing onto the jagged shore.

"Look." The giant frozen puddles.

"Look." The empty road, as if the entire island had been deserted. It felt as if we'd reached the end of the world.

But then we'd see, from off in the distance, a car on the approach. This would jolt us back into reality. Reminding us that, yes, this is a real place. We're not alone here. Our cars would pass, the other driver lifting his hand in a friendly wave. Anthony would return the wave, but a split second too late. By then, the other car had already passed into our rear-view mirror.

He turned and gave me a sheepish smile. I knew what he was thinking. We're not used to this.

Every so often, we'd pass a tiny cluster of faded saltbox cottages. I tried to imagine living in one of those homes, with kilometres-long stretches between my house and the next. I thought about all the steps it had taken to get here: a ferry to Newfoundland, a long drive to the northeast coast. An airplane to Fogo Island.

Eventually the cottages and fishing shacks edged closer and closer together. The highway was reaching an end. We had reached the village of Fogo.

We turned left onto the main street, passing a small inn and a pharmacy. The road curved to follow the shoreline. So too did the buildings, facing in every which direction. It was the largest town on the island, but really, was just a ramble of white-washed buildings—a few dozen at most, clustered around the harbour.

Consulting his GPS, Anthony turned onto an even smaller road that stretched out to the edge of Fogo Harbour. We were inching along now, gawking at the remoteness of it all.

Even so, I didn't even notice it at first. With its white clapboard siding and dark gabled roof, the restaurant looked like all of the other buildings that made up the village. But just as we were about to pass it, I spotted the faded Pepsi sign hanging above the door. It was the same sign I had seen before in pictures. "Kwang Tung Restaurant," it read in black wonton-style font.

We parked out front and I paused for a moment, looking at the building. It was almost noon but there was no "Open" sign on the door. The windows, dressed with simple lace curtains, looked dark from the outside. The restaurant looked like it might be closed. But I reached toward the door and the knob turned easily in my hand. The door opened with a start and I walked inside.

The dining room was empty. The room felt stark, with linoleum floors and walls painted light grey. The only attempts at decor were the red tablecloths covered with sheets of clear vinyl, as well as a few wooden hangings on the wall. In the front room, a small window had been cut out of the drywall, for passing takeout orders through.

I walked farther into the dining room and could hear the sound of a range hood roaring, a metal spatula clanging against steel. The kitchen started about halfway through the dining room. It was separated from the dining room with just a sliding accordion door.

From there, I could see a middle-aged woman with short black hair, dressed in a red sweater and a pink crocheted vest. It was the owner, Feng Zhu Huang. With her back turned to me and the range hood roaring in the background, she was frying up a plate of chow mein. Her gold earrings swayed back and forth as she worked.

· · · · · ·

She held my business card in her hand, rubbing the thick paper between her fingers. She could talk to me, she said, but only between customers.

By then, a pair of women had followed us into the restaurant and sat at a table at the back of the dining room. Ms. Huang wandered off to take their orders. I could hear them talking, the two white women speaking quickly in easy, casual English. Ms. Huang, in response, was sparing. "Yes," "no" and "okay." She never used more words than necessary.

Meanwhile, Anthony and I sat at a table just outside the kitchen, waiting. She returned to our table a few minutes later. "Why do you want to talk to me?" she asked. With each answer I gave her, she seemed more and more puzzled. She spoke in Cantonese with a Toisanese accent—that singsong lilt that made every sentence sound like a question.

"You came all the way to Fogo Island—to see me?" She scrunched her forehead. The idea that I was interested in her story was baffling to her. She left us with a chuckle, and returned to the kitchen to cook the women's orders.

For a few minutes, Anthony and I sat in silence. I fiddled with my tape recorder while he played with his phone. From the back of the dining room, we could hear the two women talking quietly.

A few minutes later, Ms. Huang walked by with two plates heaping with food. She placed them in front of the two women, then passed us again to return to the kitchen. As she walked by, she glanced at us again, amused. Again, she chuckled quietly.

A few minutes after that, she returned to our table, this

time with our food. By this point, we had had at least a dozen variations of Cantonese chow mein. I leaned in, inspecting the various components: the glistening water chestnuts, the candy-coloured shrimp, the bright red barbecued pork. Anthony dutifully reached for the knife and spoon, heaping a mountain of noodles onto his plate. I thought I detected a small sigh as he leaned over to take his first bite.

Ms. Huang lingered at our table instead of rushing back into the kitchen.

"Okay," she said, "what do you want to know?"

She stood there for a few minutes like that, alternating between answering my questions and making clucking noises at Anthony for not eating quickly enough.

"Who helps you run this restaurant?" I asked.

"Nobody."

"Who lives here with you?"

"Nobody."

"How is your English?"

"Not great."

"Are you the only Chinese person on Fogo?"

"Pretty much."

"How did you wind up here?"

To this point, she had responded to all of my questions matter-of-factly. But to the last question, she scrunched her face and sighed. "It's a long story," she said.

Another customer walked in, a tall man with a ruddy face and muddy boots. She wandered off to seat him and to take his order.

This time, as she passed us, I asked to follow her into the kitchen.

She shrugged. "Sure, why not?"

The kitchen was laid out in a square room. The woks and the refrigerators were along the edges, and Ms. Huang's workspace in the middle. She talked as she worked, pulling seafood out of the freezer to defrost. Stirring a bubbling red sauce on the stove. Washing some vegetables in the sink.

She described the house she grew up in back in China. Just like my family, she was from Toisan—the same *siyup* county where Ye Ye, Dad and so many of the Gold Mountain men had been from.

It wasn't a bad house she grew up in, compared to some of the others. Hers had tile floors, not concrete or dirt, like Dad's. She too worked as a farmer. She figured that would be her life.

By her mid-twenties, Ms. Huang was married with two daughters. But one day, her younger daughter, Stacey, got sick. They weren't sure what was wrong with the toddler. The doctor at the medical centre near the village thought maybe a blood vessel or an artery was infected. Then Stacey fell into a coma.

They didn't have money to send her to a proper hospital in a city like Guangzhou. For days, they agonized in the village medical centre, feeling helpless. Even after Stacey eventually gained consciousness and recovered, they were still shaken by the incident.

"We have to do better for our kids," Ms. Huang said to her husband.

His brother was already living in Canada, running a restaurant in a place called "Fogo." So they decided to follow in his footsteps.

· · · · · · ·

When Ms. Huang arrived at the St. John's airport with her husband and two daughters, she felt as if they'd landed on another planet. She couldn't understand what anybody was saying. She couldn't understand the signs posted everywhere.

They went to retrieve their suitcases from the young baggage handler. The man rubbed his fingers together, the universal sign for "tip." They stared awkwardly at him until Mr. Huang realized, a few moments too late, what the man wanted. He fumbled around in his pockets for his wallet, too embarrassed to study the crisp bill before handing it to the young man.

In Fogo, Ms. Huang followed as her brother-in-law led them toward the little weather-beaten wood house where they would be living. She hadn't known what to expect of this place, but she had expected more than this. The little house was barely a step up from their place in Toisan. But once inside, she said, "it was so nice." She laughed. There was wall-to-wall carpet. Walls finished with drywall. "It was so beautiful," she said. "So strange."

For the first while, the family stayed together in that house. Mr. and Mrs. Huang helped to run their brother's Fogo restaurant. And the couple had a third child, a son—Richard, their very own "Fogo boy." But then Ms. Huang's husband heard about an opportunity to own their own restaurant in Twillingate. This was their chance to start their own business. The whole idea of coming to Canada was to invest in themselves, to take advantage of new opportunities. So the family moved to Twillingate.

231

But a few years after that, Ms. Huang's brother-in-law decided he was ready to retire. He asked if they wanted to take over the Fogo restaurant. The couple talked it over. The restaurant in Twillingate was doing well, so it didn't make sense to shut it down. But the Fogo restaurant was a good investment too. It was one of the only restaurants on the island and there was always a steady stream of customers. They knew it would be profitable.

So they decided. Two restaurants meant two incomes. Mr. Huang would stay in Twillingate and keep running the restaurant there. Ms. Huang and the children would move back to Fogo, and she would run the restaurant there.

It wasn't ideal, but they grew accustomed to it. Like the families of the Gold Mountain men, the Huangs would live apart. Only instead of being split across continents, the Huangs were split by the harbour.

Mr. Huang would come to visit his family when he could—the odd weekend for a day or two. The rest of the time Ms. Huang was kept busy running the restaurant and taking care of the three kids. As the kids grew older, they would help out at the restaurant too, doing their homework in the dining room and taking breaks to help Ms. Huang take orders, or clean dishes.

Eventually, it was time for the kids to leave too. Kacy moved to Halifax, where she works as an accountant. Stacey moved to Vancouver, then to Toronto to work as a physical therapist at a private health clinic. And then even Ms. Huang's "Fogo boy" went off to university in St. John's.

Now, she was alone.

I still couldn't wrap my head around it. What did she do all day to pass the time?

She shrugged. "I work," she said. Matter-of-factly.

Each day, from morning until night, she worked at the restaurant.

When the restaurant closed, she'd do some preparations for the next day—making sure the ingredients were defrosting in the refrigerator, checking to make sure the supplies were all there.

Then she'd cook herself a simple meal, some steamed vegetables and white rice, and eat it quickly in the empty restaurant, or take it into her apartment.

Sometimes she'd watch television. Or take a shower.

And then it was time for bed.

"Every day is like this," she said.

Did she have friends on the island?

She thought about it.

"One friend," she said. A man who dated a woman who used to work in the restaurant. Sometimes he would come by and help fix things around the restaurant. Like the water filter, when it was acting up and the taps filled the water glasses with green-looking water. It tasted fine, but was alarming to her customers, so she called him and he took care of it.

And there was that one time she got sick. It was the one and only time she had to close the restaurant. He was the one who came and found her. "I saw the restaurant was closed," he said to her. "I knew right away something was wrong."

She chuckled, shaking her head as she recalled his alarmed expression. "I knew right away something was wrong," she repeated.

"So what do you do on your days off?"

She gave me a strange look. "The restaurant is open every

single day," she said. "Three hundred and sixty-five days a year." There were no days off.

The longer we talked, the more baffled I felt.

She didn't have a cellphone.

She rarely left the restaurant.

She had no car, so she hardly left the tiny village.

There was no sadness in her voice. Every response she gave was just a statement of fact.

Even after the Fogo Island Inn opened a few years ago, with its daily room rates of over $1,600 suddenly thrusting the tiny island into the spotlight, Ms. Huang still hadn't made it to the other side of the island to see it.

She just shrugged.

"My husband showed me a photo of it once," she said. The sparkling steel-and-glass box sitting atop stilts and overlooking the ocean.

"I thought it looked pretty nice," she said.

She took in the astonishment on my face and laughed. "My life is simple," she explained. "But for me, it's satisfying."

• • • • • • •

The two women at the back of the restaurant signalled for their cheque, and Ms. Huang shuffled off toward them. For a few moments I was left alone in her kitchen.

I glanced around the room where she spent so much of her time. The room was dimly lit. The sink, where a bowl of frozen seafood was defrosting. The sound of the range hood, still roaring in the background.

In the kitchen there was a can of root beer sitting on the table. As Ms. Huang walked, she would wander over to the table every so often and take a long sip from the can. Each time, she let out a contented sigh.

"My life is simple," she had said. Simple pleasures.

I remembered the peanuts my dad would rustle out of a bag and into a bowl some nights after dinner. He'd sit in his lounger, one eye on the TV, another on the bowl. He'd crack the peanuts one at a time with his teeth. That satisfying pop ringing in our ears. He'd tilt them out of their shells and into his mouth, chewing slowly. The crumbly shells he'd discard into a paper napkin. The salt he'd lick off his fingers. Looking back, it was one of his only indulgences that I can remember.

• • • • • • •

After a while, the restaurant picked up again with customers, and I rejoined Anthony in the dining room. He was still picking away at the plate of chow mein. I picked up a fork and began eating too. The noodles had grown cold, but they were still crunchy.

Ms. Huang eyed us each time she passed. "That's it?" she said, tsking at the small helping on my plate. Her eyes widened, an attempt to intimidate. "You should eat more!"

The phone rang and she rushed back into the kitchen. This had already happened a number of times throughout our visit. Each time, the phone would ring and she'd excuse herself. "Hello restaurant," she said each time into the phone. At first, I assumed they were customers calling in their orders. But each time, she would switch to Cantonese soon after. I realized they were friends, or relatives.

When she returned to our table, I asked her if it was normal for her to receive so many calls in a day.

She hesitated. She seemed to be mulling something over. Whether or not to tell me something.

A few seconds later, she gave a small nod, as if willing herself to continue.

"Today is my birthday," she said quietly. She used Cantonese slang for "birthday," literally translating into "cow" and "one," because the characters, when combined, form the Chinese word for "birth."

"My fifty-fifth."

That was why the phone kept ringing. Her relatives from across Canada and China were all calling to wish her a happy birthday.

She smiled shyly.

I was startled. By then, we'd already been talking for well over an hour.

I turned toward Anthony, translating quickly what she'd just said. "It's her birthday," I said. His eyes widened in surprise.

"Happy birthday," he said to her quickly.

"Happy birthday," I repeated in Cantonese.

I asked her what she had planned for the day.

But Ms. Huang only shrugged.

"I work," she said. Originally her husband had planned to come for a visit. But just as we had been derailed by the storm—and the lack of ferry service—so too had he.

She shrugged her shoulders again, as if to say, *No big deal.*

"It's just a birthday."

"Will you have cake to celebrate?"

She just laughed, as if the idea was outrageous.

"It's just like any other day," she said. "I'll have dinner after work."

"By yourself?"

"By myself."

"What will you eat?"

"There's a free-range chicken in the freezer that my husband brought on a previous visit," she said. "I've been saving it for a special occasion."

Each time she answered, I translated what she'd said for Anthony. I could see his eyes darting back and forth, looking at her, then imploringly at me. I could tell that he was thinking the same thing as I was, and wondering what we should do.

Ms. Huang looked at both of us, once again taking in our astonished expressions. She paused for a few moments again. It seemed she wanted to gather her thoughts.

This was all *normal* to her, she explained. "Of course I think about him. And of course I miss them," she said of her husband and family. But for them, this made sense. It worked for them.

Anyway, her days of living like this were numbered. The kids were trying to persuade them to shut down one of the restaurants.

"They don't like me being here by myself." She let out a small laugh. The thought seemed to make her happy. "They say I'm getting older, and if anything happens, nobody will know."

When the restaurant began clearing out, I asked if she could show me her apartment. She seemed reluctant, but agreed all the same. "There's not much to see," she said, leading me down a cluttered hallway. She opened a door and walked into a room filled with stacks and stacks of spare light bulbs, Styrofoam takeout containers and other restaurant supplies. Behind all the storage was a couch and a television. It was her living room.

Just like the restaurant behind us, the space was sparingly decorated. Here, she allowed for a few framed photos. Some pictures from Stacey's graduation. "This is when she got her master's," Ms. Huang said proudly. "That's Kacy," she said pointing at another photo. "At a formal."

Richard had just graduated from university, she said. "I should put a picture of him up too. Hopefully, he'll have a job soon," she added.

It reminded me of something she'd said just minutes earlier, in the restaurant. Just moments after I told her about my own dad, and how he'd run a restaurant when we were growing up, she'd nodded, lost in thought.

"This is what we do," she had said. "We work, work, work until the kids all have jobs. That's when we stop working."

• • • • • • •

A short while later, we pulled out of the Kwang Tung parking lot and turned back toward the main street. Both of us were silent, lost in thought. Ms. Huang's words were seared into my brain.

"My life is simple."

"You think I'm crazy."

"Today is my birthday."

We drove slowly, following the road to the tip of the coast, then circled back in the direction we'd come. We passed the restaurant again and made our way back onto Main Street. We passed an inn and then a drug store. When I saw a convenience store, I grabbed Anthony's arm. "Stop," I said.

"Here?"

I told him I wanted to grab something quickly and stepped out of the car.

In the store, the shelves were piled high with knick-knacks and bags of potato chips. I had hoped to find a birthday cake, but there wasn't even fresh bread, let alone a bakery section. Finally, I spotted by the cash register a large, round tub of Moritz Icy Squares chocolates. I picked up the tub, pausing to wipe the dust off my fingertips. The price tag read $6.99.

It wasn't much. But it was something.

Back at Kwang Tung, Ms. Huang was in the kitchen. Once again, she was on the phone.

I waved at her from the doorway, and she looked at me, surprised.

"Hold on a minute," I heard her say into the phone in Cantonese.

"It's not a cake," I said, handing the chocolates to her. "But happy birthday."

She stared at the chocolates in her hand, in disbelief. A goofy grin spread across her face. Eventually, she threw her head back and laughed. She looked genuinely thrilled.

"Thank you!" she said, following me as I headed back out the door. "Thank you!"

Simple pleasures, I told myself.

• • • • • • •

The next morning, we parked our tiny Fiat in the lot beside the St. John's International Airport. The car, originally white, was now coated in a thick layer of grime. The dirty slush from the Coquihalla Highway, the dust from the Prairies and the grey sludge from the Nova Scotia snowstorm clung to every surface. The lettering on our front plate, "Beautiful British Columbia," was completely covered in soot.

After eighteen days on the road and 9,625 kilometres, we had completed our journey and were ready to fly home to Toronto. We had eaten more spring rolls and plates of chow mein than I cared to think about. I had a folder in my suitcase filled with the menus of Chinese restaurants we had visited from coast to coast.

As we made our way toward the terminal, I thought about the questions I had set out to answer with this journey. One question—whether these chop suey restaurants were still operating, and whether the tradition of "fake" Chinese still existed—that one had been answered pretty quickly. It had been clear the moment we set foot in Amy's, back in Vulcan, that the tradition was not only continuing, but thriving.

Another question I'd been hoping to answer: What brought them here? When I'd first set out on this trip, I'd imagined the stories we might hear. Thinking about the size and scale of this country, and of the many thousands of Chinese who have wound up here, I had imagined the stories would differ dramatically. In many ways, they had. The stories had ranged from heartbreaking to awe-inspiring.

But then I thought about the families we'd wound up meeting. I thought about Mayor Choy's mother, Jean, how she had clasped both my hands in hers, speaking to me in Toisanese and sending us off with a huge grin. There was Mr. Yu, the Deer Lake restaurant owner who grinned when he spoke about his daughter in university. And Ms. Huang, describing her sick toddler. Their stories of what brought them here and why, I realized, were all the same. And all along, the question I'd been looking to answer had been wrong.

It wasn't *what* they came for, but *who*.

Burnaby, BC.

December 2016

OWARD THE END of December, Dad was growing restless. He was getting tired of my questions. It was starting to feel like I was asking the same things over and over again, without clear answers.

There was one question in particular he was never able to properly answer: Why had he been left behind all those years ago?

At times, his responses were vague. Once he told me it was because of rules surrounding his residency. Because Dad had lived in Guangzhou, at a different address from Ah Ngeen in the village, she wasn't able to do their applications together. But that didn't explain the thirteen-year delay. Another time, he told me Ye Ye and Ah Ngeen *had* made earlier attempts to bring him to Canada, but that some administrative complication had come up. He didn't explain what that complication was. Another time, it was something different altogether. He mumbled something about "buying papers." But, when pressed, he wouldn't elaborate further.

Mom had given me yet another answer. And so too had one of my aunts. Nobody seemed quite clear on the details.

Because of Dad's evasive replies, I couldn't figure out whether he didn't want to talk about it, or whether there were still details even he didn't know.

So I drove out to an elementary school in Burnaby to see my Aunt Janice. There was still snow on the ground, and the roads were icy. I made my way gingerly up the sidewalk, climbing a set of stairs toward a blue door. Inside, the walls were covered with brightly coloured drawings and student photographs. From the classrooms came the sounds of kids tittering, of teachers trying to speak over them. I looked around me until I spotted a sign pointing to "Administration"—the principal's office. Aunt Janice's office.

Aunt Janice is the older of Dad's two younger sisters, born fifteen years after him. Looking at her and my dad, it sometimes seemed inconceivable that they were siblings. Their lives and upbringing had been so different. Aunt Janice greeted me in the hallway, wearing fleece pants covered with Santa Clauses, and a necklace made of Christmas lights. I looked around the office and saw that others were wearing bathrobes and flannel too. "It's pajama day," she said by way of explanation. Unlike my dad, who always seemed lost in thought, Aunt Janice had a lightness to her. She was clever and always quick with a laugh.

She invited me into her office, and as we sat down, I explained the questions I was trying to answer. I told her that none of us, including Dad, seemed to know much about Ye Ye's first years in Canada.

She nodded slowly. "He really didn't talk about it much," she said.

"He didn't talk to you about his life in China?"

"Not really," she said.

"Or about his first few years here?"

She shook her head. She told me about how Ye Ye had worked on Great-Aunt's farm for the first few years, growing Chinese vegetables, bok choy and choy sum, to be trucked into Chinatown. Eventually he left to work for himself as a carpenter in Chinatown. He developed a reputation for his craftsmanship and became known as the unofficial carpenter for Chinatown restaurants. The Hong Kong Cafe (where the *original* apple tarts were created). Foo's Ho Ho Restaurant, with its neon blue-and-red sign. Ming's, the splashy banquet restaurant on Pender. They were all clients of Ye Ye's. When Mom and Dad had their wedding banquet at Ming's, they ate off round red-and-black tables that Ye Ye had built by hand.

Aunt Janice's memories of Ye Ye rounded out Dad's descriptions. She saw the strict, stubborn side—how he would lose his temper, once throwing their plastic Christmas tree in the garbage because Janice and Jennie took too long to put it away. But she also knew the charismatic side: the Ye Ye who loved to tell jokes and charm his clients into becoming regulars. She told me about how he loved the Chinese opera and volunteered his time building sets. He would take her and Jennie along to job sites on the weekends and feed them apple tarts while he was working.

I asked why she thought he was so reluctant to talk about his past. I told her it was the same with my dad.

"Do you think it's specific to our family?" I asked.

She thought about it before shaking her head no.

I wondered whether it was cultural—whether it was a Chinese idea. Perhaps it was tied to *Ga chou but ho ngoi yeung*—the idiom that translates, roughly, to "don't spread your family's troubles." Perhaps they saw some kind of shame in talking about their struggles.

She shook her head again, thinking it over. She suspected it might be generational.

"I think that generation just felt like, what's happened, happened," she said. "They didn't see the point in dwelling on the past. They just wanted to move forward."

Then she added another idea, one I had never considered before. Maybe it was their way of protecting us from the trauma that they'd been through. Maybe they wanted to keep our lives untouched by the pain of their pasts.

Aunt Janice had kids too, my cousins Matthew and Cameron. I could tell she was thinking about them as she said this. She was nodding her head now. She seemed to understand it better than I ever could.

• • • • • • •

Almost an hour after I'd first arrived in her office, Aunt Janice mentioned three words that stopped me in my tracks.

She was talking about Ye Ye's arrival in Canada, and Great-Aunt's help in getting him here. Before I knew it I heard her say the same thing Dad had said once before: "Bought the papers."

I stopped her. "What does that mean?"

"You know he bought papers from Great-Aunt, right?"

It was roughly what Dad had said once before. But when I'd asked him to explain, he had shut down the conversation. I had assumed he was referring to a payment Ye Ye gave to Great-Aunt to help cover the cost of sponsoring his immigration.

"Yes, but what does that mean?"

She explained how she had stumbled across the papers as a kid. They were documents for Ye Ye—citizenship papers, and health records. But some of the documents had different names on them. Some had his given name: Hui Man Yen. But others had a different name altogether: Wong Mun Goot. It was a name she'd never heard before.

Confused, she asked Ye Ye and Ah Ngeen about it.

"That was my name before," Ye Ye told her.

Before what?

Gradually, it all came out. Great-Aunt's offer to Ye Ye had come with one major condition. He'd had to give up his own identity.

"He was a paper son," Aunt Janice said to me.

As soon as she said this, I let out a small breath.

I'd heard the term before. I'd learned about "paper sons" in history class, and come across it countless times in my research. After the head tax, and later the Chinese Exclusion Act, it was nearly impossible for Chinese to enter Canada—the first and only time the country excluded an entire group based solely on race. Even after the act was lifted in 1947, immigration was open only to the spouses and children of Chinese already in Canada. I'd read about how this led some Chinese who were desperate to come to Canada to do so illegally and "buy the papers" of those who were already here. How citizenship documents for husbands and sons and nephews were bought and sold to those desperate enough to pay hundreds or even thousands of dollars for them.

Each time I'd read accounts of these events, they had felt so distant, so far removed from my own life. I'd always thought they were the stories of the *lo wah kew*, the early Chinese-Canadians whose family names were engraved on Chinatown buildings. The events felt like chapters from a long-ago past. Never had I imagined any of it had touched our own family.

"So who was Wong Mun Goot?" I asked Aunt Janice.

She shrugged. She'd heard he was Great-Aunt's son, but that he'd returned to China for a visit, and gotten into some kind of trouble. She'd heard that maybe he was in jail there. But in truth, she wasn't sure. "No one really told us," she said. "There were only stories."

Back at home, I asked Dad about it.

As soon as I said the words "bought his papers" and "paper sons," he let out a long sigh. It seemed as if he'd been dreading this conversation.

"Did you know Ye Ye was a paper son?"

Dad nodded his head slowly. For his first few years in Canada, everyone was hushed about it. But eventually Dad had pieced it together. That was the reason the family had split up.

Ye Ye had come to Canada as Wong Mun Goot, a bachelor. That was why he'd left Ah Ngeen and Dad behind.

When he finally brought over Ah Ngeen, he was only able to

do so because he'd applied for her as his girlfriend, not his wife.

"Do you remember that photo I showed you?" Dad asked. That black-and-white photo of Ye Ye and Ah Ngeen all dressed up. The first time he saw Ye Ye's face.

That photo, he explained, had been their "wedding photo." They had staged a fake wedding to make their marriage official in Canada.

This was why they'd had to leave Dad behind. Neither of their fake identities in Canada accounted for a son. According to the Canadian government, Dad didn't even exist. It was only later, after the government granted amnesty to these "paper sons," that they could finally give up the charade. Between 1960 and 1972, about 12,000 Chinese came forward to the Canadian government about their real identities and have their status "adjusted." It was only after Ye Ye and Ah Ngeen had confessed that they were finally able to bring Dad to Canada, legally.

I listened as he told me all of this, letting his words sink in.

Wong Mun Goot.

Fake identities.

A fake wedding.

I didn't even exist.

It started to make sense to me why Ye Ye and Ah Ngeen had stayed quiet about it for so long, and why Ye Ye and Dad were never able to clear the air about it.

Ye Ye and Ah Ngeen had spent decades living as ghosts. For almost twenty years, they had lived in the shadows, in the lives of other people. They had grown used to hiding. Whether it was out of shame, or habit, even after they'd "confessed," they still kept hiding.

I asked Dad the same thing I'd asked Aunt Janice.

"Wong Mun Goot. Do you know who he was?"

He said he had heard different stories from different people.

"I think he died," he said.

A few moments later, he changed his mind.

"Maybe he never even existed to begin with." Then, he added, "No one really knows."

I was stunned by all of it. By what Aunt Janice had told me. By what Dad was now telling me. He loved this country more than almost anyone I knew. Every Canada Day, he put a Canada flag the size of a sofa in our front yard. Anywhere he went, he wore a little maple leaf pin proudly displayed on his baseball cap.

And yet. Ye Ye's entry into Canada, which paved the way for Dad and all of the rest of us—it had all started with a lie. All of it had been built on a fake name, on a piece of paper and a man who might have never even existed.

• • • • • • •

It snowed the night before I was scheduled to visit Dad's uncle, Sook Gong. It had also snowed the night before that, and the night before that. There were giant piles of snow everywhere, piled high on the side of the roads and covering the sidewalks with grey slush and sleet.

We'd had to cancel a family dinner because of the weather. Pansy's car wasn't able to make it up the steep hill leading up to Mom and Dad's house. Dad looked forward to these weekly Sunday night dinners. Plus, he was feeling the effects of the latest round of chemo. He'd napped pretty much all day and was still tired. It frustrated him.

"Why don't you just reschedule?" he asked grumpily. He didn't want me driving to Sook Gong's in the snow. "You could always go next week."

I told him I had a strict schedule and deadline. "There are still things I don't understand. Things about Ye Ye that only Sook Gong might know."

"Well, then I'll come with you," he said. "Then I can drive."

I sighed. I suspected there was more to his objection than a concern for safety. In the days since I'd spoken with Aunt Janice, it had become clear how much Dad still didn't know. I could tell he was curious to hear what Sook Gong had to share. Dad had gone from reluctantly answering my questions to eagerly participating.

So the next morning, we set off in the Toyota hatchback toward my great-uncle's house in South Vancouver. We pulled up outside the house, with its red-brick exterior and cream-coloured vinyl siding. It had been over a decade since I'd last been here. But as Great-Uncle swung open the door and led us into the foyer, I marvelled at how little it had changed.

The house is a "Vancouver special," an architectural style popularized in the 1980s and 1990s and designed to maximize every square inch of living space out of Vancouver's neat, square lots. Just about every relative and Chinese family we knew growing up lived in one of these Vancouver specials. Not only were the houses cheap to build, they allowed for a downstairs suite, which meant grandparents or extended families could all live under the same roof.

Sook Gong led us up the stairs and down the hallway, where the carpets were covered with clear plastic mats. He took us into the kitchen and sat us down next to a box of pineapple buns he had bought that morning from a Chinese bakery down the street. He had just returned home from dropping the grandkids off at school, he said—his way of apologizing that he hadn't yet prepared tea. As he spoke, he dug around the cupboards, looking for plates, then looking for a kettle to fill with water.

While he did this, I looked from Dad to Sook Gong and back again. I could see how, growing up in Guangzhou, the two had easily passed as brothers. But while Dad arrived in Canada in 1974, Sook Gong had to wait fifteen years longer. He arrived in Vancouver as a middle-aged adult. He came with a wife and three kids to support. Unlike Dad, who had a little bit of time to settle in and learn English, Sook Gong had to get to work right away. He spent decades working at a produce shop in Chinatown before eventually retiring.

We spoke, as always, in Cantonese. Mine stilted, his with just a trace of a Toisanese accent.

"What do you want to know?" he asked.

"I want to know why Ye Ye left his family behind."

Sook Gong nodded. He was quiet for a long moment, and I could see Dad stirring in the corner. "People did what they had to do back then," he finally said.

"Did he write letters?"

"Yes, every year," he said. "He would write a letter and send some money back." That was what kept Ah Gong, Bak Bak, Ah Ngeen, Sook Gong and Dad afloat.

"What did the letters say?"

"He told us not to *gwa sum*." *Gwa sum*—hang our hearts. Worry.

Sook Gong had only been a toddler when Ye Ye left. I asked him about everyone who had been left behind.

"Your parents—Bak Bak and Ah Gong. Did they miss him?"

He was quiet again, then opened his mouth to speak. But instead of words, he let out a choked sound. He began slowly shaking his head, back and forth.

"Of course—"

He could still see Bak Bak's face when she received the letters.

Dad was staring at Sook Gong, listening intently.

Sook Gong continued. Tears began streaming down his face. The words tumbling out in fits and starts.

"We were so poor."

"There wasn't enough to eat."

Ah Gong wasn't able to support them. Ye Ye thought he could.

"He had to do what was best for our family."

"He was only in his twenties."

"It was so hard for him."

Dad wasn't the only one who had sacrificed. Ye Ye had sacrificed too.

And then Sook Gong said the words Dad had waited to hear, what he may have gradually come to understand, but that Ye Ye had never said out loud.

"He had no choice," Sook Gong finally said. "He did the best he could."

I looked to Dad, expecting him to jump in or to cut Sook Gong off. Tears normally made Dad uncomfortable.

But instead, Dad lowered his eyes, as if he couldn't bear to watch.

In the background, the refrigerator was buzzing. Somewhere off in the distance, the sound of children playing outside.

The two of them sat there without speaking. They sat there, in shared silence and in shared grief.

Toronto, ON.

January 2017

*I*N A CROWDED Starbucks in the underground mall beneath Toronto's Financial District, I sat waiting. It was late January, and each time someone walked into the coffee shop, I looked up, scanning their face.

But instead of Stacey Huang, it was another man dressed in an immaculate suit. Or a group of women in pencil skirts with giant purses, their heels sparkling despite the snow and slush outside. Students with lumpy backpacks, cutting through the mall on their way to campus.

I checked the inbox on my phone.

"I'm wearing a pink shirt and a white sweater," she had emailed to say. So far, no one there matched the description.

I checked my phone again. 3:35 p.m. She was five minutes late.

I was feeling anxious. It had taken almost two months to arrange this meeting with Stacey. And many months before that to track down her email address and work up the nerve to contact her. Stacey was the daughter of Ms. Huang from Fogo Island—the young woman who, as a toddler, had been hospitalized in Toisan. She was the Huangs' second-born, who grew up on Fogo Island and moved to Toronto after university.

The road trip article had appeared in *The Globe and Mail* in June 2016. It had been published with a large photo of Ms. Huang, and her story had been featured prominently in the piece. Afterward, I'd sent a copy of the paper to Ms. Huang. I hadn't expected to hear back and never did. In the months following, I often wondered what she'd thought of the story. I wondered what her kids thought. Time after time, I'd thought to myself about how I would feel if I were in their shoes.

I understood what it was like having immigrant parents— parents with imperfect English. I knew the responsibility of fending off pushy salespeople at the door. I knew the feeling of seeing my parents rendered temporarily helpless by a cashier, or a bank teller, or a government letter. I tried to imagine how I would feel if I'd heard a reporter had shown up at their door, and then I'd woken up to find their story and all the bare details of their lives exposed in a national newspaper. I worried that I had betrayed her mother, especially now that I realized I'd revealed so little of myself.

But when Stacey finally wrote back to me, she was kind. "I'd be happy to chat with you," she said. It took a few more weeks of back-and-forth to pin down a date. She was travelling, and then I was travelling. Each time she took more than a few days to respond to my emails, I would start to worry. "Maybe she's read the story again," I said to myself. Maybe she'd decided it was awful. Or that I was awful.

I was anxious to talk to Stacey for a lot of reasons. I wanted to hear what she and her mom thought of the story, and whether there was an update on the family's situation, whether they were still running both restaurants, and if Ms. Huang was still running the Fogo restaurant alone. I was also curious to meet Ms. Huang's daughter. Ms. Huang's story had left me deeply moved, and I wondered what the experience had been like for her children.

There were other questions I hoped Stacey might help answer. By now, it had been nearly a year since my initial visit to Fogo. In the many months in between, I had discovered how closely her family's story paralleled my own. Standing there in the Kwang Tung Restaurant a year earlier, Ms. Huang's experience had seemed so alien. And now I knew our family's stories were in many ways the same.

Just as I reached down to check my phone again, I spotted a young woman entering the shop. She had long, straight black hair. A white cardigan and a pink shirt. Stacey. I walked up to greet her, pausing to shake her hand. She had a round face with the same narrow eyes and high cheekbones as her mother. It almost felt like I already knew her.

"You look just like your mother," I told her.

She responded with a laugh. She'd heard it countless times before.

• • • • • • •

"I was like, 'It makes it sound so sad,'" Stacey said, with a little laugh. "And you happened to be there on her birthday." Her

257

voice trailed off. She was describing reading her mom's story in the paper for the first time.

She'd been living in Toronto for the past two years. As soon as she graduated with her master's degree, she moved out to Vancouver for a job. She lived and worked there for a few years before coming to Toronto. Here, she worked on the thirtieth floor of the gleaming office tower above us. She was a physiotherapist, treating executives and athletes at an elite private clinic.

Talking to her here, just another smartly dressed young woman in the middle of downtown Toronto, seemed like an impossible juxtaposition with my meeting with her mother. I tried but failed to conjure up the image of that faded restaurant on the quiet island where she'd grown up.

"It just made her sound like the loneliest person on the planet," she said in a quiet voice.

She thought for a while.

A lot of her parents' choices might strike others as odd, Stacey said. The decision to live separately the way they did, the decision to work 365 days a year and never close their restaurants. The fact that they never, ever spent any money on themselves.

"My mom would wear out her shoes," she said. "Same as my dad. He owned, like, four items of clothes and washed them constantly."

It reminded me of my own parents.

I told her about my parents and their dishcloths. And about how, even a decade after I'd moved out, I'd still find my mom wearing hand-me-downs, not from other relatives or friends, but from *us*. The clothes they had bought us as teenagers—studded T-shirts and brightly coloured Gap parkas we'd long since discarded—my mom was now wearing as her own.

Stacey nodded in recognition. These were decisions they had made, she said, and they were content with them. "My mom's never, ever shown me any signs of regret," she said. "She's never like, 'I wish I had done this instead.'"

Despite the challenges of living in Fogo, Stacey said, the life they'd built there was still better than what they would have had in China. For all of them.

But things had changed since my last visit, Stacey told me. Her younger brother, Richard, had recently moved back in.

My heart lifted. "So she's no longer living alone?" I asked.

"Not for now," Stacey said. Richard had just graduated from university and was figuring out his next move. Until then, he was living in the apartment with his mom and helping out at the restaurant.

And there was more.

She told me how, a few months earlier, her mom had called her, asking for a favour.

"Your auntie just bought a house in a new development in Oshawa," Ms. Huang said to her. "She said we should buy one too. Can you go look at it?"

Stacey was surprised. Her parents had talked about retiring near Toronto. But they'd always talked about it as something in the far-off, distant future. It never seemed serious. They'd also never before mentioned Oshawa, about an hour's drive away.

"Just go look at it," Ms. Huang said.

So Stacey agreed. What was the harm in looking?

At eight a.m. on the morning that Stacey planned to set off for Oshawa, she received a phone call from her mother's friend—the auntie who had recently bought a house in the same development.

"I'm in line at the developer's," the auntie told her. "I saved you a place in line."

Stacey was confused. "I thought the office didn't open until eleven," she said. "Line?"

"Just get down here," the woman said.

When Stacey arrived, there was a huge line wrapped around the developer's offices. Her auntie waved frantically from the front. Moments later, when the doors opened, a saleswoman began rattling off information. Stacey hadn't known what to expect, but she hadn't expected this. The Toronto-area real estate market was in the middle of a major boom, and suddenly she was thrust to the very forefront of it. For decades, prices had inched up and then, in the past year, skyrocketed— especially in suburban areas like Oshawa. Houses were being bought sight unseen, while others sold in frantic bidding wars for hundreds of thousands of dollars over their asking price. The saleswoman pressured Stacey to make a decision.

"We have four plots available," the woman said. She pointed to maps and layouts on the wall. "Here, here, here and here. Which do you want?"

Stacey was overwhelmed. She'd thought she was there to look at pictures and maybe take home a brochure. She picked up her phone and called her mom.

"They said there are only four houses left," she told her. "They say we have to buy one now or they're going to sell out." She added, quickly, "We can always wait for the next phase to come out."

But her mom barely hesitated. "Well," she said, impatiently, "just buy one then."

So they bought a house. A brand-new, four-bedroom, detached house. It has a backyard, a front lawn and a basement.

Once it's built, Mr. and Mrs. Huang will wind down their two restaurants. They'll retire and move in, living together for the first time in decades. Their daughter will be just an hour away. The picture-perfect retirement they'd always dreamed of.

Bitter first, sweet later.

. . . .

It was nearing the end of the workday and the cafe swelled with more and more people. Beside Stacey and me, the espresso machine hissed and gurgled, exhaling long breaths of steam. By then, we'd been sitting for almost an hour. There was still something I wasn't sure how to ask.

I explained to her the larger purpose behind our meeting. I told her about learning about my own family's connection to Chinese restaurants. How I was trying to understand my dad's history and how I hoped it might help me better understand him.

"My dad's sick," I said finally. I told her how he'd been slowing down. How he'd been skipping more of his Saturday hikes. How sometimes, when he answered the phone, he seemed to barely have enough energy to answer my questions.

I spoke slowly, unsure of how to proceed. "I guess what I'm trying to figure out is, what now?"

I knew I was being unclear. So I continued.

Her parents, like mine, had spent all their lives sacrificing. They had scrimped and saved for decades, giving it all to their kids. I recounted to Stacey how, even after my family had moved out of Abbotsford—even after Dad had become head chef at a big restaurant in Vancouver—the sacrifices never stopped. I told her how, when Expo 86 came to Vancouver, my dad took a side job supervising the overnight kitchen operations at Cara, which was catering several of the pavilions. Each day, he'd work a full day at the restaurant, then report for the night shift at Cara at around ten p.m. From there, he'd work until morning, overseeing the kitchen line. Afterward, he'd drive straight back to the restaurant, napping for just a few hours before he started work all over again.

Stacey nodded, listening. A few times, her eyes flickered with recognition.

I told her how, as I was growing up, Dad often had two, three, even four different jobs—restaurant, contracting and landscaping jobs—working evenings, weekends and all hours of the day. Eventually, he'd retired. But he'd never stopped scrimping.

"So now, here we are," I said, gesturing around me at my five-dollar latte, at the crowd of women in their shiny heels and the men with their briefcases, at the gleaming office towers above us with their marble foyers and contemporary art collections. This place we were both living in that felt worlds away from the lives of our parents.

She just kept nodding. She seemed to understand what I was getting at.

I wanted to ask her about dealing with the guilt. And the question of how we could ever repay them.

But instead I settled on this: "How do you know if you're living up to the expectations?"

The question didn't seem to throw her. It seemed like something she'd thought about before.

"These days," she said, "it's about making sure my parents are comfortable." She's offered to help put her brother through grad school if it will help her parents to retire sooner. She's offered to help them financially too.

Beyond that, she said, "You just don't want to disappoint them."

I asked her what that meant—what she or her siblings could have done to disappoint them—but she shook her head.

There weren't specific expectations, she said. They weren't told they had to become doctors and lawyers and accountants. (Even though initially, she did want to become a doctor. And her sister went on to become an accountant.) There wasn't pressure to be any of that.

"There was a very strong indicator that we should make money. I mean, I don't think I've ever been encouraged to be a writer," she said, looking up quickly at me.

I laughed. I said I wasn't pressured either. I'd had lots of friends who had struggled with that growing up, arguing with their parents over career directions and fighting over what they saw as their parents' single-minded view of success. But I didn't blame the immigrant parents who tried to force their

263

kids into these careers either. Many did so out of fear. They wanted stability for their kids, and they saw in these labels and letters, MD or LLD or PhD, a kind of protection.

For Stacey, her parents just wanted to make sure she'd be able to take care of herself. For years after she moved to Vancouver, and then later to Toronto, the questions her dad asked her during their phone calls were all the same: "Do you have enough to eat? Do you have enough money? Are you doing okay?"

I thought back to all the conversations I'd had even over the past few months with my dad. All of the weekly phone calls with the both of them from Toronto.

"Have you eaten?" they would ask. "How's work?" To each of their questions, I would grunt a yes. That was more or less all that was ever said. Underlining those conversations was always a simple question: *Are you okay?* Even after all this time, they were still worried.

But recently, Stacey said, she'd managed to get them to understand that she's not just getting by, but doing well. The clinic she works at is a branch of one of the leading hospitals in all of North America. She's paid well and lives comfortably. She has her own apartment in downtown Toronto and travels frequently. Now they can be at ease, she said.

"Instead of, 'Do you have enough?' now he's like, 'You've got to take care of yourself, you've got to pace yourself,'" she said, laughing.

"It's interesting," she said. "He recently asked me—and he's never, ever asked me this question before."

I asked what it was.

"He asked me if I was happy."

The espresso machine let out a loud hiss as I sat there, thinking about what she'd just said.

He asked me if I was happy.

She chuckled. She knew it was unusual, and the question had surprised even her.

"So how did you respond?" I asked.

"I was like, 'All right, yeah. I'm happy,'" she said. She smiled as she said it. We were underground, underneath harsh lighting, but she glowed as she said it. And I believed her.

Her mom had called recently, Stacey said. She'd said something that had stuck with Stacey. It echoed the words Ms. Huang had told me back in Fogo.

"My mom said to me, 'We can breathe now. You kids are okay. We can breathe now.'"

CHAPTER TWENTY-FOUR

Burnaby, BC.

March 2017

*T*HE FIRST MESSAGE came on a Thursday evening.

It was a text from Pansy. "Hey Ann. We met with the home nurse and Dad isn't doing well at all," it read. "They are taking Dad to the Burnaby Hospital right now. Amber and Mom are with Dad."

The messages kept getting worse.

"Dad's tumours have grown and spread."

"Palliative care."

On the phone, Pansy recited the long lists of procedures Dad had been through. They repeated the same jargon the doctors had used. "But what does that mean?" I would say, over and over. No one ever seemed to know.

This, I had learned, was the language of cancer. People would ask how Dad was doing, and I'd stumble. I knew what they were really asking: *Is he doing better or worse? How much longer does he have?* But we didn't have answers to these questions. So just like my sisters, I would recite the procedures and symptoms. I'd repeat, word-for-word, the latest updates from the doctors, knowing full well I wasn't telling them what they wanted to hear.

Eventually Amber said the words I'd been dreading: "You should get here as soon as possible."

It was nighttime when I arrived at the hospital from the airport. No one had told him that I'd be coming. They weren't sure when I'd arrive and worried I wouldn't make it in time. They didn't want to get his hopes up.

The hallways were flooded with fluorescent light. My heels clicked noisily as I made my way toward palliative care. As I neared the room, I realized that I was terrified. The last time I'd seen my dad, he'd acted like everything was fine. He was walking slower and taking more naps, but we'd still been able to pretend like everything was normal. Now, I didn't know what to expect.

"He's here," Pansy said quietly, gesturing toward his room. It was a room in the corner, across from the nurse's station.

Inside, Dad was lying in the bed, his eyes closed. He looked thinner and was wearing a hospital gown. I don't know why that surprised me. But I thought, *Oh, he's wearing a hospital gown.*

I must have made a sound, because he stirred in the bed. His eyes rested on me. He nodded but didn't speak. I walked over and put my hand in his. He clasped back tightly.

I hugged him gingerly, afraid of jostling the tubes in his arms. Normally when I hugged him—each time I said goodbye at the airport—his entire body would stiffen. Hugging wasn't natural for either of us, and he never quite knew what to do.

But on this day, he submitted. I pulled away, and he grabbed a tissue to dab at his eyes. I'd never seen him cry before, and I wondered what that meant. Was he happy to see me? Was it grief? Did he see in me some sort of a grim reaper—that my arrival was a sign that his own end was very near?

On TV and in the movies, death seems dramatic. There's always a flurry of activity. A beeping noise that suddenly becomes insistent. A vital signs monitor goes flat. We're fooled into thinking that dying is linear and definitive. That most of all, it's quick.

In reality, those days at the hospital were mostly dull. They were slow. Day after day, we waited. At times, Dad was awake and alert, eager to flip through old family photo albums or tap on his iPad. Visitors would come and go. Sometimes he would sit up to talk with them.

Other times, he would lie there with his eyes closed, only letting out a chuckle every once in a while to let us know he was still there and listening. On those days, I sat and stared. He would sleep and I would watch. My mind would drift, and I'd find myself noticing the smallest details. His skin stretching across his arms—forming parallel lines, like bar codes. In my memories, my dad's arms were dark and muscular. Now they were thin and pale. Other moments, I would simply sit and stare at the bed linens. I would get angry, then try to understand why. Angry at the bed sheets. Angry at the machine that beeped every time Dad moved his arm even a little. Angry at the nurses for taking so long to come by to readjust the tubes.

Yet he never seemed angry. He told me so, over and over again.

On his good days, we talked about some of the stories he'd

recounted for me in the past few months. About growing up in China. About coming to Canada. About the restaurants he'd opened. About Ye Ye. About the mountains he'd faced.

"I have no regrets. I lived a full life," he told me.

In the quiet moments, I remembered my conversation with Stacey. About her parents and what she owed them. What brought them comfort.

"We're okay," I tried to tell him. That he'd given us everything we needed. "All of us are okay." Anthony and I in Toronto. My sisters. Our mom.

"We're going to be okay," I said, over and over.

• • • • • • •

It happened several weeks later. He got a little bit better, and then a little bit sicker. And then we lost him.

I was back in Toronto that day, so the news came from my sisters. "It happened this morning," Amber told me over the phone.

The week after that passed like a blur. Another flight. My sisters picking me up from the terminal. The Taiwanese beef noodle shop we stopped at on the way back from the airport. Phone calls with the funeral home. Tracking down documents. Putting things in boxes.

He had been dying for over a year and a half. In that time, I had been grieving every single day. While I stood in line for coffee. When I sat down in front of my computer. On the bus home from work. It had been there during our phone calls, and during those visits home. In every conversation we had, and in every question I asked. Even as he sat there, living, I had been grieving.

Now that it was over, all we had were boxes. Bags. Unopened crates of crystal tableware. Kitchen equipment that hadn't been touched for decades. Bottles and bottles of Johnnie Walker and Courvoisier XO—gifts he'd received and saved over the years. The blanket wrapped in plastic. Rooms full of things he had spent decades storing away. Remnants of a life spent saving.

Dad didn't want a funeral. He'd spent enough time sitting through ceremonies and sermons. He knew we'd spent enough time grieving. He wanted a celebration.

So at the very end of the week, we all gathered—Mom, my sisters, Aunts Janice and Jennie, Sook Gong and all of our cousins. All of the closest family and friends who had come together in Dad's last days. We met for dim sum at Dad's favourite restaurant. From his cellar, Amber and I had picked the nicest bottle of cognac. We poured it into teacups, passing it around the tables.

We told them that it was from one of the bottles Dad had been saving. And then we all raised our glasses to toast.

• • • • • • •

The most lasting memory I have of my dad—before the hospitals, before the wheelchair and the IVs and medical tubes—was from a December day we decided to drive back to Abbotsford.

It had been years since Mom and I had been in Abbotsford. When I was growing up, we would all take annual trips back around Christmas to visit their old friends. But those visits tapered off over the years. Eventually, Dad was the only one who still made the trip, checking up on their rental properties and collecting rent from tenants. But shortly after Dad got sick, he'd sold the Abbotsford houses. And now he hadn't been for over a year either.

I myself was curious to visit. Now that I knew more about their Abbotsford lives, I wanted to see the streets with those stories in mind. I wanted to see their apartment on Pauline Street, the Park Inn and the Legion.

So that morning, we jumped into the car. Dad insisted on driving. But as he switched on the windshield wipers to clear away the snow, something caught his eye. One of the wipers was broken—the top had snapped off from the bottom. I turned and looked at him, as if to say, *What now?*

Without a word, Dad opened the car door and walked back toward the house. I turned around and looked at Mom, sitting in the back seat. She looked back at me and shrugged. A few moments later, Dad emerged from the house. He had a roll of packing tape in his hand.

With one hand, he held the two pieces of the wiper together. With the other, he secured the two pieces together with an elastic band. Then he took the packing tape, wrapping it around and around and around until the wipers held together. He got back into the car, and I tried to maintain a straight face.

"Um, Dad. Do you think that's safe?"

He turned to me and nodded with complete confidence. "It's fine," he said. "It's not even snowing anymore."

"Yeah, but—"

He interrupted, lifting his hand in a dismissive wave. "I'll go to the garage later," he said. "This is just for now. To get to Abbotsford."

It was typical Dad. He'd find ways to fix just about anything using whatever he had on hand. Sometimes it was a coat hanger. Other times it was packing tape. Relatives jokingly nicknamed him MacGyver. He was the master of making the best of what he had.

On the highway, Dad pointed to the landmarks that he remembered.

"On this side," he said, pointing at a forested spot like any other lining the highway, "is where the people digging gold would go to sell." We were in Fort Langley, near the site of one of the first Fraser Valley gold discoveries in the 1850s. In that time, over thirty thousand men poured into the area in search of gold.

As we continued on Highway 1, I eyed the speedometer nervously. Over the past decade, Dad's driving had grown slower, more cautious, to the point where I'd sometimes have to remind him, gently, "Dad, you're driving thirty on a fifty road." If it was one of us behind the wheel, he'd clutch the handle above the passenger side window nervously, shooting us disapproving looks. But today, as he sped farther and farther away from Vancouver, I watched the speedometer teeter near 120—fast enough to blow past dirt-encrusted trucks on the road.

I wondered if it was muscle memory, from all those days and nights when he'd race back and forth between the cities. All of those Sunday nights over the years, speeding back after a visit with Po Po or Ah Ngeen, with two exhausted toddlers in the back seat.

So I didn't say anything. Dad was energized, more excited than I'd seen in months. He was talking faster, his head swivelling back and forth as he drove. We passed sprawling farmland, abandoned trailers. I asked him what he thought of this place when he first saw it in the 1970s. After all, he had only just arrived a few years earlier in Vancouver, eager to adopt the city and all of its cosmopolitan amenities.

But Dad shrugged. "I spent a lot of time on farms growing up," he said, "I was used to it. Dirt ground. Growing stuff. I was used to it."

But did coming out to Abbotsford feel like taking a step back?

"No," he said. "I knew we wouldn't be here for long." He figured they'd stay for ten years, tops. It reminded me of what Ms. Li in Boissevain had said to me—about life being made up of many decades.

"It was just what we had to do," Dad said.

We were getting closer. Abbotsford was twenty-two kilometres away, a sign read. Not long after, another sign: "Abbotsford: City in the Country."

Dad pointed to a sprawling suburban-style development looking out of place amid the farmland. "That's new," he said. From the back seat, Mom gawked at a giant new shopping complex on our left, with a Cineplex theatre and an H&M store. "None of this was here before," she said. "It was just hills."

We veered off at the exit, past warehouses selling farm

equipment and seeds, and drove beneath a billboard advertising the Abbotsford Agrifair.

"You see that liquor store?" Dad asked a few minutes later, as we drove down one downtown street. "That's where the other Chinese restaurant, the Fraser Valley Inn, was." He was talking about another Chinese restaurant that later opened up in Abbotsford.

We drove toward Astoria Crescent—the street where we lived in Abbotsford. He pointed to a stretch of highway. "There used to be more trees here," he said. "The deer would be running back and forth." He pointed to an ice rink. "That's where we used to take you guys skating—we bought you skates here," he said.

Then he turned onto a quiet suburban street. He slowed to a stop next to a white split-level with dark blue trim. This was the house where they'd lived when I was born. I had no recollection of it. "They took out my siding," Dad said, rolling down the window to take a closer look. The ice-cold air hit our faces, jolting us awake after the long drive. He nodded in approval. A set of white icicle lights hung from the trim and a dark Pontiac sedan sat parked in the driveway.

I tried to remember living in this house. This was where I would have spent the first year of my life. All I could come up with were the images from our photo albums. The picture of Pansy and Amber building a snowman on the front lawn, using navel oranges on his belly in place of buttons. The picture of me taking my first wobbly steps on the carpet, my chubby knees peeping out beneath a polka-dotted dress.

With a sigh, Dad rolled up the window. He was ready to

move on. He turned the car around, heading back toward old downtown.

After turning off McCallum Road at McDougall Avenue, he took a sudden left onto Pauline Street. Near the corner was a grey stone building designed to look like a medieval castle. The windows were shaded by green-and-white striped awnings. "Dragon Fort," the sign said in bright red lettering. It was a giant, new-looking Chinese restaurant. Dad all but ignored it, instead pointing to the empty lot next to it. It wasn't clear if it was a parking lot or just vacant. The lot was mostly paved over, with just a few small patches of grass sprouting up here and there. A dumpster was placed in the centre.

"This is where our first apartment was," he said.

We continued down the same street. He slowed to a park outside a grey-brick Travelodge.

He squinted at the sign on the side of the building. "Yok—yuk yuk?" he said.

"Yuk Yuk's," I said. "It's a comedy club."

But he'd stopped listening. He'd already opened his driver's side door and was halfway out, barrelling toward the Travelodge. I followed, confused. Mom trailed us both, a few steps behind. I still wasn't sure why we had parked here, why Dad was so intent on being here. Suddenly Dad stopped in the middle of the sidewalk. Pointing at one side of the hotel, which was now being used as a liquor store, he turned and looked at me. "That's where the restaurant was."

"Wait," I called out as he rushed ahead. "This was... the Park Inn?"

But Dad was already headed inside, pulling open the wooden

doors to reveal a gleaming lobby with tile floors and crystal chandeliers overhead. When I caught up, he was already talking to the young receptionist at the front desk. The building had been a Travelodge for at least a few years, I heard her say. The owners before that were the same people to whom the hotel had been sold when my parents left.

We chatted with her a few minutes, asking about the area and the building.

"Is the downstairs still a banquet hall?" Dad asked.

She nodded.

"Is the place across the street still a bar?" he asked.

"It's the Townhall," she said. Still a bar, just a fancier one, with craft brews and a gluten-free menu.

"Sometimes, when I would come back to Abbotsford for a visit, I would go there for a beer," my dad said. "I was hoping I might run into my old customers."

We walked around the corner, carefully avoiding the patches of ice on the sidewalk. On our left, we passed a small park. "I used to take Pansy here," Mom said quietly. A few seconds later, we slowed again to a stop, this time in front of a beige brick and stucco building.

"This is it," Dad said. "The Legion." Mom looked up in surprise. She looked at Dad, then back at the building again. She looked confused.

The original building that housed the old Legion had been taken down, he said. Now there was a new building. On one side of the building was a Subway restaurant. On the other, roughly where the Legion had once been, was a sushi restaurant. Its name, "Kojan," was spelled out in big block letters.

The restaurant was at the edge of the brick plaza. It was still late morning and the parking spaces in front of it were empty. The fluorescent "Open" sign wasn't yet lit. Out front was a middle-aged woman with short black hair, carrying a bucket. It looked as if she was about to start cleaning the windows and glass door. I approached her and asked if she was the owner. She looked confused. I wasn't sure if she'd understood me after she turned around and walked back into the restaurant, leaving Mom and Dad and I standing outside in the cold.

But a few moments later, a different woman with youthful skin who wore a puffy vest came out to meet me. She introduced herself as Ruth Park. I explained to her why we were there. I pointed to my parents and told her how they used to run the restaurant on this same site. English was Ruth's second language, so it took a few minutes before the puzzled expression disappeared from her face.

"Ahhh," she said eventually. A large grin spread across her face. She extended her hand toward Dad, and he shook it.

"1976," I said. "That's when they opened their restaurant."

She nodded, impressed. She invited us inside—an offer Dad declined. He hadn't entirely recovered from walking in the cold, it seemed. He said he'd rest with Mom instead in the car.

So I followed Ms. Park into the restaurant. It was a large dining room, with dozens of tables scattered across the floor and a row of booths along one side. There were a few of the usual signs of a Japanese restaurant—a sushi bar against the back wall flanked by paintings of cherry blossoms. But the rest of the dining room was decorated in shades of burnt amber and terracotta, and with dark wood furniture. It looked Mediterranean.

"This used to be an Italian restaurant," Ms. Park said. Her family had taken over the space less than two years earlier, converting it to a Japanese restaurant. She had no idea about the history of the property before that. She didn't know that the property had once been a Legion, or that there had once been a Chinese restaurant here. She'd never before heard of the Legion Cafe.

Ms. Park's family was from South Korea, she said. They'd been in Canada since 2002, when her husband, a pastor, began studying at Trinity Western, a Christian university in nearby Langley. A few of their friends in Korea had been to Canada before and told them it was a good place for a sojourn. The original plan had been to return to Korea after his studies, she said. But by that time, their two sons, now twenty-two and twenty-five, were reaching middle school. "It felt like it was too late to go back to Korea," she said. They decided instead to stay in Canada.

I asked if she liked living in Canada.

"Both good and bad," she said.

What was the good?

"In Korea, everybody—the relationships are very close," she said. Her English was good enough to get by, but hesitant. She spoke slowly.

"Everyone is always watching you, asking questions. Here, I feel freer."

I nodded. Ms. Huang had said something similar on Fogo. And that was part of the reason Mom and Dad had left Vancouver for Abbotsford. It was part of the reason I'd left Vancouver all those years earlier for Toronto. To get away from expectations. To build a life I thought was entirely mine.

As we sat talking at one of the tables, a young man stood behind the sushi counter, slicing bright green avocados for lunch service.

She gestured toward him as she spoke. Her son, she said. "In Korea, there's so much competition in studying. You have to study hard and pay fees," she said. The schools here were better for her sons. They loved it here.

We sat talking for a few more minutes, until a family of customers walked in just before noon. Ms. Park perked up, smiling at the customers and walking over to speak briefly with the servers. She pushed some buttons on the cash register, getting the business started for the day. She had to get back to work, and I took that as my cue to leave.

"Thank you," I said to her before I left. There were other things I wanted to say. I wanted to offer her some assurance that the gamble that she and her husband had made would pay off. I wanted to tell her that it had worked out for my own parents and my own family. That maybe there was still some good luck to be found on this site.

But I couldn't promise her any of that. I didn't know whether this would work out for her family. For every family that found Gold Mountain, there were many others who didn't. There were the many faded restaurants I had visited that seemed on the verge of shutting down. There were towns where one after another, the storefronts were shuttered. Where the restaurant owners greeted me with glum faces. The owners who shook their heads, *no,* when I asked to hear their stories. The ones who seemed ashamed to be found.

I had no idea whether it was hard work, or timing, or just

good luck that might lead to success for Ms. Park and her family. Perhaps they'd already found it. Perhaps this restaurant, and the lives they were already leading in Abbotsford, were exactly what they'd been looking for. So instead I just thanked her, again and again. "Good luck," I said as I headed out the door. I meant it.

Soon after, we were back in the car, heading to Vancouver on Highway 1. As we sped toward the city, we passed under a railway bridge with a green sign: "CP Rail."

"The cycle just goes on and on and on," I said to Dad. I relayed back to him what Ms. Park had told me. I told him about how she and her husband had come from Korea, how they'd decided to stay for their sons. I told him how she didn't say it, but I could tell how difficult it must have been for her. How I couldn't pretend to understand, but only try to imagine how difficult it must have been, learning a new language and trying to build a new life in a new country. How much I admired her.

He nodded, but stayed silent. I couldn't tell if he was tired, or thinking.

He looked ahead and just kept driving.

He was speeding ahead, the speedometer ticking danger-ously above the limit. Anxious to be home.

From the rear-view mirror, a glint. The mountains behind us, catching us the light.

"They're so beautiful," my mom gasped, craning her neck to look out the back window. She was right.

Beneath the snowcaps were the trees that had made it through the long cold winter. They had since lost their leaves and the bare branches reached up and out toward the sun.

They were shining amber. With the light bouncing off them, they looked as if they'd been set ablaze.

From a distance, from where we were they looked as if they were made of gold.

Acknowledgements

THIS BOOK WAS made possible by the many restaurant owners across Canada who generously gave their time and opened up their lives to a complete stranger. I am especially grateful to Qin Lin at Amy's in Vulcan, Linda Xie and Peter Li at the Diana in Drumheller, Kwong Cheung at the Silver Inn in Calgary, William Choy at Bing's #1 in Stony Plain, Lan Huynh at Thai Woks N'go in Glendon, Jeff Deng at Panda Garden in Bonnyville, Su Fen Li at Choy's in Boissevain, Norina Karschti at Ling Lee's in Thunder Bay, Gen Le at Saigon's Garden in Nackawic, Gah-Ning Tang, Jae Chong and Eun-jung Lee at Korean Restaurant/Acadia Pizza & Donair in Dieppe, Allen Huang at Huang Family Restaurant in Glace Bay, Richard Yu at the Canton in Deer Lake and the Huang family: to Stacey and Feng Zhu.

This book could not have been written without the support of *The Globe and Mail*. The original "Chop Suey Nation" article that appeared in the *Globe* was the result of the efforts of many, including Denise Balkissoon, Melanie Morassutti, Gabe Gonda, Kevin Siu, Mason Wright, Cliff Lee, Alison Gzowski, Ming Wong and Ben Barrett-Forrest. I'm also indebted to National Editor Christine Brousseau for her unending patience and for giving me the time to pursue projects like this one, and to the entire national desk: Nicole MacIntyre, Madeleine White and Hayley Mick. I'm also thankful for the support from many editors over the years: Dennis Choquette, Angela Murphy, Jim Sheppard, Stephen Northfield, Sinclair Stewart and David Walmsley.

My thanks to the team at Douglas and McIntyre: Anna Comfort O'Keeffe for her support, Nicola Goshulak for thoughtful guidance and Brianna Cerkiewicz for her detailed edits. Many thanks to my agents John Pearce and Chris Casuccio at Westwood Creative Artists, who believed in this book even when I didn't. And thanks to colleague Elizabeth Renzetti for introducing us.

I am also grateful to Henry Yu at the University of British Columbia, to Linda Tzang at the Royal Alberta Museum, to Ian Mosby, and to Lily Cho at York University, for their research assistance, and to Lloyd Bailey in Fogo Island for his help along the way.

So many friends and colleagues contributed their thoughts throughout this project. In particular, Hannah Sung and Lisan Jutras, who were kind enough to read early drafts. I'm also thankful to Dakshana Bascaramurty, Charmaine Sue, Elim Chu, Melissa Stasiuk, Robyn Doolittle and Katherine Scarrow, who offered advice and words of encouragement. Many thanks also to my friends and fellow reporters: Caroline Alphonso,

Jill Mahoney, Patrick White, Molly Hayes, Joe Friesen, Eric Andrew-Gee, Tim Kiladze, Tu Thanh Ha, Marcus Gee, Ivan Semeniuk, Sean Fine, Renata D'Aliesio, Kathryn Blaze-Baum, Greg McArthur, Colin Freeze, Oliver Moore and Kelly Grant.

I am especially grateful to my family: Janice Nakatsu (and Allen, Matthew and Cameron); Jennie Jung (and Stan, Taylor and Connor); Hui Chu Chi and family; Chow Hoi Chow (and Teresa Chow, Denise and Foster Yee, Bonnie Loo and Varian Loo, Edmond Chow and Andria Lam); and to Ken and Ada Tsang (and Michael, Tonia and Michelle).

And finally, thanks to Anthony, the most patient travel companion I could have asked for. And to my mom, Frances Hui, and sisters Pansy Hui and Amber Hui, for trusting me with Dad's story.

Select Bibliography

Cho, Lily. *Eating Chinese: Culture on the Menu in Small Town Canada*. Toronto: University of Toronto Press, 2010.

CHOW: Making the Chinese American Restaurant collection. Museum of Food and Drink, Brooklyn, NY.

Coe, Andrew. *Chop Suey: A Cultural History of Chinese Food in the United States*. New York, Oxford University Press, 2009.

Harley J. Spiller menu collection. University of Toronto Scarborough Library, Archives & Special Collections.

Hui, Ann. "Chop Suey Nation." *The Globe and Mail*, June 21, 2016. https://www.theglobeandmail.com/life/food-and-wine/chop-suey-nation/article30539419/.

Imogene Lim Restaurant menu collection. Vancouver Island University, Special Collections, Nanaimo, BC. https://viurrspace.ca/handle/10613/2695.

Kaori. "Part 2: I Can't Believe There's a Chinese Restaurant in Fogo." *I Can't Believe I'm Back in Toronto* (blog), June 25, 2018. http://icantbelieveimbackintoronto. blogspot.com/2008/06/part-2-i-cant-believe-theres -chinese.html.

Lee, Jennifer 8. *The Fortune Cookie Chronicles: Adventures in the World of Chinese Food.* New York, Twelve: 2008.

Mosby, Ian. "That Won-Ton Soup Headache": The Chinese Restaurant Syndrome, MSG and the Making of American Food, 1968–1980. *Social History of Medicine,* 22, issue 1 (April 1, 2009): 133–151. https://doi.org/10.1093/shm /hkn098.

Thakray, Maureen, and Carole Taylor. Letter to Vancouver city councillor Carole Taylor on "monster home" debate, August 5, 1988. City Clerk's operational subject files. City of Vancouver Archives, Vancouver, BC.

University of British Columbia. "Chinese Canadian Stories: Uncommon Histories from a Common Past." October 13, 2010. http://chinesecanadian.ubc.ca.

University of British Columbia Library. "The Chinese Experience in British Columbia: 1850–1950." Accessed August 30, 2018. https://www.library.ubc.ca/chineseinbc /index.html.

University of British Columbia Library. "Immigration and Settlement." Accessed August 30, 2018. http://chung .library.ubc.ca/collection-themes/immigration-and -settlement.

Yee, Paul. "History of Canada's early Chinese immigrants." Library and Archives Canada. Last modified April 19, 2017. https://www.bac-lac.gc.ca/eng/discover/immigration /history-ethnic-cultural/early-chinese-canadians/Pages /history.aspx.

Yip Family Collection. Museum of Vancouver, Vancouver, BC.

Yu, Henry. "Global Migrants and the New Pacific Canada." *International Journal* 64, issue 4 (December 1, 2009): 1011–1026. https://doi.org/10.1177/002070200906400410.